HOMEOSTASIS

THE JOURNEY OF A MANIC-DEPRESSIVE

DONALD RODRIGUEZ,
PENELOPE RODRIGUEZ

Copyright © 2016 Donald Rodriguez, Penelope Rodriguez.
Cover Image by Ana Rinaldi.

All rights reserved. No part of this book may be reproduced, stored, or transmitted by any means—whether auditory, graphic, mechanical, or electronic—without written permission of both publisher and author, except in the case of brief excerpts used in critical articles and reviews. Unauthorized reproduction of any part of this work is illegal and is punishable by law.

This book is a work of non-fiction. Unless otherwise noted, the author and the publisher make no explicit guarantees as to the accuracy of the information contained in this book and in some cases, names of people and places have been altered to protect their privacy.

ISBN: 978-1-4834-6330-8 (sc)
ISBN: 978-1-4834-6329-2 (e)

Library of Congress Control Number: 2016921092

Because of the dynamic nature of the Internet, any web addresses or links contained in this book may have changed since publication and may no longer be valid. The views expressed in this work are solely those of the author and do not necessarily reflect the views of the publisher, and the publisher hereby disclaims any responsibility for them.

Any people depicted in stock imagery provided by Thinkstock are models, and such images are being used for illustrative purposes only.
Certain stock imagery © Thinkstock.

Lulu Publishing Services rev. date: 12/21/2016

Acknowledgments

Thank you to the Mat-Su Valley, Alaska, K-9 Unit and Search and Rescue Team. Without their dedicated and unrelenting efforts to find me, this story would not be possible.

Thank you to my family and, most important, my mother, whose selfless compassion has been more than enough to keep me going.

Thank you to my friends for always being there and keeping me (in)sane.

Homeostasis: the body's ability to keep most internal bodily processes within normal limits, despite the variety of changes that happen externally.

Preface
THE APOLOGY FOR MY MANIC BEHAVIOR

Originally, I began to write while in the throes of a manic episode, the kind where you have delusions of grandeur, lose contact with reality, and really piss off everyone around you. I wrote obscenities that were not indicative or consistent with who I was as a person and said things I should not have said. To all of those I hurt, scared, or angered, I apologize for my manic behavior.

The worst part about being manic is you can't understand what's happening to your mind or realize the impact of your behavior until you do something that harms you or someone around you. I put my friends and family through hell before they were able to eventually find help for me. I nearly lost my life in the process. And now I see that there's a light at the end of any tunnel you go through, no matter how endless and dark it may be—although there are times when I pray that that light isn't another train headed my way.

Homeostasis started out as a collection of some of the essays I wrote while manic. I've included a few of them at the end of this book. Through these pieces, I intended to encourage readers to find balance in life. Now the story is about how I work to reach my own homeostasis.

Part 1

THE AFFERENT SIGNAL

Chapter 1
DECEIT, DEMENTIA, AND DEPRESSION

Sobbing, I sit alone in my car in the garage, engine idling. My parents are in Miami to visit my sister. My brother lives in New York. No one is here to stop me, should I decide to end my young life right now. It's the spring of my junior year in high school, and I had just cheated on my girlfriend of five years last night—impulsive. Someone told her, of course, and now she is furious and has broken up with me. Everyone at school knows. I'm consumed with guilt, and swear I will not go back to school. Cannot go back. The exhaust starts to creep into my consciousness. I consider just staying put and letting the carbon monoxide do its thing. Instead, I back out of the garage and head up to the North Shore to visit my grandma. She will take me in. She will make things right.

I have never driven up I-35 from St. Paul to Duluth by myself before. Through my stupor, I have enough sense to pack my dog and his leash so he won't be left alone unattended. I don't know how long I'll be gone. But that's where my good sense ends. The sky grows dark, and I have no idea where the turnoff from Highway 61 to Stoney Point is. By now, I've passed through Two Harbors and am several miles beyond my destination. Even in the dark, the shoreline is beautiful. Waves crash gently against black granite rocks, gleaming under the dim light of a quarter-moon that shines across the vastness of Lake Superior. They always seem to calm me down. I call my mother, and she guides me back to Gramma's.

My grandma knows I'm coming, so she has my two comfort foods—pizza and frozen yogurt—ready for me. Once I settle in, I look around her small home that had once been a summer cabin, and I notice things aren't right. Papers and boxes are everywhere. Books are stacked on tables and other furniture. Nothing is in its place. The floors look as though she hasn't vacuumed in months. A thick layer of dust covers everything. My grandma asks me the same questions over and over again. Slowly it begins to dawn on me that my once sassy and brilliant grandmother is showing signs of dementia. No one else in my family realizes this yet, and I am devastated by what is sure to come.

    I don't sleep soundly that night. The next day, I spend some time sitting by the lake, letting the steady rhythm of the waves wash away some of my despair. Then I pack up my bag and my dog and head home. A gray veil slowly descends over me. I can feel the seeds of depression begin to take root. I lost, and am about to lose, two of the most important people in my life.

Chapter 2
LOWER-BODY INJURY

Our biggest game of the year. The private vs. public school rivalry we all have been waiting for. Us, being the public, versus them, the private. We sit in the locker room that Saturday morning, waiting for the coach to tell us the ice is ready. Being the goalie, I lead the team down the walkway and onto the ice. Normally I would be nervous, but for this game, we have nothing to lose. They always beat us. The question just becomes, how bad? For me, it's personal. The other team is loaded with friends who are former teammates from a AAA Bantam team I anchored during our freshman year. I know their moves, and they know mine. We do a couple of laps before starting the warm-up. Then the helmets come off for the national anthem, and we're ready to drop the puck.

The first period, a shot from the point. Pad save. A shot from the circle. Blocker save. Another shot from the point, pad save, rebound, glove save. That's mostly how the game goes for us. The private school team spends the majority of the game attacking us. I stand as the last line of defense to an onslaught of shots. A couple of big saves and more routine ones leave the game at 5–0. They outshoot us 67–12. A reporter from a local newspaper interviews me after the game to talk about my performance. He summed it up in one sentence: Rodriguez "saw more rubber tonight than you see on I-35 during rush hour." But you know hockey; it's all about the team. Luckily for everybody, I am in the zone.

I have a 4–1 record heading into this game with two shutouts. This game sounds like nothing special, but it was for me. That was my school's best loss to this team in decades. It instilled the confidence in me and my team that we could play with anyone, even the defending back-to-back state champions. We knew we didn't have much of a chance at this game, but it was early in the season, and we had plenty more to go. At least that's what I thought.

We have a tournament up north in Eveleth soon after. We travel by bus up through lake country to the region known as "the Iron Range." All the way there, we laugh and play jokes on each other, the usual stuff teenage boys do to build team spirit. We arrive at the motel and unpack before heading over to the rink for our first game. We enter the yellow-and-green arena and make our way to the visitors' locker room, the one that looks like a 1970s gym locker room. Right skate, left skate, right pad, left pad, chest protector, jersey, helmet, glove blocker, stick. The routine is always the same for a goalie; we are a superstitious lot. My team and I get ready to take the ice.

First period in, the game is tied 1–1. We are outplaying this team, and they only score on a lucky power-play goal from the lower-right hash mark. Then all of a sudden, an odd-man rush comes out of nowhere. It's a two-on-one with a back-checker just lagging behind. They charge toward me. That's when things get hazy. I get thrown from the net and twisted up on the post. I feel the pain, but I don't know what happened. I try to get up but find that I can't put any pressure on my left ankle. I know I'm out for the game, but the question is, how long will I be out?

Someone takes me to the local hospital, and initially the doctor says it's just a high ankle bruise and I should be good to go. Wrong. I try playing again, only to find that I can't go down to stop a puck, so I'm done. I see an orthopedic specialist when I return home and learn to my dismay that I have torn all the ligaments in my ankle and have chipped off a piece of bone. My senior year playing hockey is over. I have to rehabilitate my ankle a lot to get it back to normal.

I train hard over the spring and manage to get back on the ice, but the magic isn't there. I haven't skated in months, let alone worked out. I am the fattest I've ever been and devastated from losing out on my option to play college hockey. I skate hard all summer, hoping to try out for a junior team in Canada before deciding I am not ready. In fact, I come to the sad conclusion that I will never be ready. Instead, I opt to go to school, depressed that I will not be pursuing my childhood dream.

Chapter 3
COLLEGE

I roll over and look out onto the Charles River rippling toward the city of Boston. The famous Citgo sign, Fenway Park, and the Prudential Center come into view. Sunlight filters through a narrow window that shines brightly over my twin-sized bed. I groggily roll out of bed before checking my phone: 8:50 a.m. I have an organic chemistry final at nine o'clock only a block away. I frantically get dressed, pop my Adderall, and sprint to the elevator to make my way down from the thirteenth floor of the student dorm, not stopping for anyone. I run in between the winding pathway from one dorm to the next, taking a shortcut to ensure that I get to this final promptly. No time to wonder at the ever-present gusts of wind or to admire the gardens in full bloom around me. I can only focus on making it to this test on time. I rush through the doors, down the stairs, and abruptly stop to collect my breath before grabbing my seat for the exam. Time: 8:55 a.m. Not bad for someone who spent the last two nights studying without sleep. I begin to mildly hallucinate at this point. Adderall will do that to you. I sit down thinking I am prepared for this exam, material fresh in my mind, when all of a sudden it goes blank. I look to the girl next to me, who happens to be a study buddy of mine from the night before, and I explain my situation. She laughs and gives me the generic response of, "You'll be fine." I get a B+. Fine, but for any premed student, it has to be an A, nothing less.

I never liked going to class. Something about sitting there while a guy drones on and you have to jot down every word seemed inefficient to me. I work better on my own, a lesson I didn't appreciate until senior year. I value the expertise my professors bring to my learning, just not the usual delivery. I'm not a traditional kind of guy. I just can't focus on lectures … or much of anything that I am supposed to.

I arrived in Boston in the fall of 2011, determined to prove myself as a premed major. I loaded up on hard classes, joined a fraternity, and played for the club hockey team. In short, I took on way more than I should have. I ultimately set myself up for failure. I couldn't focus. I was tired all of the time. I finally sought help from my family physician, and we decided to try Adderall to help me focus and Trazodone to help me sleep. I dropped one class and finished pledging for my fraternity. Still I struggled. I didn't make time for the counseling that usually goes along with Adderall use. And my visits with my doctor were quick and infrequent the few times I came home during my college career.

My grades first semester were average at best, so I believed I would have to perform perfectly during the remaining semesters in order to get a med-school worthy GPA.

Much of my joy came when I played club hockey. I made some of my best friends playing with my team. They taught me valuable life lessons, including how to manage premed coursework with efforts to have my over-worked mind have a healthy body. That wasn't enough. My family physician and I decided to add Prozac to the Adderall. She believed I had situational depression based on what I told her: my grandma had just died; my high school girlfriend of several years had dumped me; college coursework was intense; I was sleep-deprived. Meanwhile, two concussions ended my club hockey career. I finally had to hang up my skates for good. That sealed the deal. Maybe my depression *was* caused by life events. But neither the Prozac nor the Adderall worked as advertised.

The worst part about Adderall is that it will make you hyper-focused but not necessarily on the thing you want to zero in on. The dark and negative thoughts creep up on you, and you can't help but dwell on them, wondering how to evade them. These thoughts take over, and it becomes impossible to think about anything else—a predicament for a premed student who needs to study, not stew.

Premed is a cutthroat environment, and I had lost the first quarter of my collegiate career. That lingering feeling of the necessity for perfection is all I could think about. I walk to and from class along Commonwealth Avenue, back to the dorms, and hear kids talk about test answers I didn't get, even though I had the material down and had tutored others in it the night before. I understood the material, mostly, but could not get it done when it came to test time, further plunging me into a hole. Looking back, the amount of Adderall, Prozac, and caffeine I routinely had in my system was lethal when test time arrived. The anxiety was overwhelming. I did not have the means or techniques to calm myself down. I only could focus on the outcome of each test and what that meant. The depression was getting worse, largely because of my stumbling academic performance at that point, and I couldn't tell anybody. Premeds don't ask for help; they solve their own issues. Compartmentalization.

I managed to get by my sophomore year—a little bit better, but still not at the level I believed necessary. The summer between sophomore and junior year, I started my first internship with a lab at an Ivy League school in Boston. There, I worked for the dean of admissions on a research project my dad helped me get.

I worked with a teammate of mine from club hockey who was also premed, and he told me about his major, which I did not know existed: human physiology. I had no idea that was even an option. I immediately switched, and that decision ended up saving my life—but I'm getting ahead of myself.

Dealing with depression is difficult, especially the stubborn kind. A fog descends over your mind, making it impossible to think—not having enough dopamine or serotonin will do that to you. It's hard to keep paralyzing thoughts all bottled up inside, as many people my age try to do, but I did a pretty good job of it. Except once.

I did consider suicide during the fall of my junior year, although contemplation was really all it ever was. I had gotten into an argument with a roommate over a girl, and I thought it would be easiest to just end it all because the situation was that messy. I believed it was just a misunderstanding, but really it was my fault. I was so distraught because I had finally found a girl I liked, but my friend had previously dated her, so he and many of my fraternity brothers resented me. I retreated to my closet to get away from my friend after breaking the news to him, and I tried to sleep, bottle of sleeping pills in hand. Trazodone, the kind that is unlikely to kill you should you take too many. My roommates fortunately took me seriously and called 911. I texted my mom, telling her she'd be hearing from my roommates, but I was fine. "Just a misunderstanding," I assured her, but it wasn't. It was then that I knew something was really wrong with my mind. I would never end my life, but I had run out of options, and instead of coming clean, I lied about it to avoid any more attention. I had handled the situation wrong, but I learned that playing with one's life is a serious offense, and it can send you to the penalty box or even give you a game misconduct.

The summer between my junior and senior year, my quest for solving the depression took a new turn.

While working in a neuroscience lab, I stumbled onto a cool new state-of-the-art method of electrically manipulating neurons in the brain. No, not electroconvulsive therapy. I have read *One Flew Over The Cuckoo's Nest*: no thanks. (That treatment method works for many people, but I wasn't ready to go that route yet.) My roommate Travis and I learned extensively about using electric current to boost brain cell activity: tDCS, or trans-cranial direct current stimulation. We knew enough to be dangerous and made our own trans-cranial stimulation device, hoping it would cure me of my depression and provide us both with supercharged brains. Clearly that did not happen.

It works by essentially raising the resting membrane potential of your neurons from about -70mV to about -40mV so that your neurons are more likely to fire. We ordered parts online and found an electrical engineering student to help set up the breadboard circuit. I don't know how we convinced him to help us make it. Anyway, we all gathered around in my apartment (there were a couple kids who wanted to see us explode) and prepared to try it out. The voltage read 0.2 mV. We placed the cathode and the anode in the supposed right places (somewhere in the prefrontal cortex on either side) and sat there for half an hour. No robust effect, although we weren't expecting one. We were still alive though, and if anything, placebo effect worked because I felt momentarily better even though I could smell my hair sizzling. This was the first time I used electrical stimulation on my brain. Did it work? Probably not. However, real tDCS has had some better results for depression. I was still depressed, and neither of us became more brilliant—no more than we already thought we were. This is what premeds do, though. They learn and experiment. We foolishly used our own brains, the most important things we possess as animals, to test our makeshift device. We did learn important lessons, though: do whatever it takes to succeed and learn for the sake of science, but leave the rest to the professionals. Yet, it is hard to succeed when your mind cannot function properly.

I managed to graduate with a decent GPA, but I believed it wasn't high enough to get me into medical school because everyone who is premed thinks that. So, I came home and took the summer off, and by off, I mean I did absolutely nothing. I'd worked hard right through my four years at school in Boston and needed a break. I also needed to come to grips with a future that might not have anything to do with my course of study in college. I needed time to study for the MCAT, the all-important test you have to take to apply to medical school, while I tried to sort out my life. I never took the test. Twice I rescheduled the exam. It's during the quarter in between these test dates that I experienced my mind operating with a clarity and speed that I had never before experienced. And then it completely shut down—both ends caused me to nearly lose my life. So often, bipolar is misdiagnosed as attention deficit disorder or major depression. The danger is the medications used to treat these disorders can actually send someone with bipolar disorder into a state of mania.[1] Turns out that's what happened to me. And self-medicating, like so many people with bipolar do, just sped up my ascent. Fast-forward to December 31, 2015.

---

[1] *Psychiatry (Edgmont)*. 2006 Oct; 3(10); 57-63. Published online 2006 Oct.

Part 2
THE INTEGRATING CENTER

Chapter 4
NEW YEARS

I am nervous but excited to see my old buddies again in New York for the New Year. On the plane from Minneapolis/St. Paul, I remember reading *Concussion* and thinking that's probably how my head will feel after this weekend. I touch down at JFK just after noon and take the subway into the city. I arrive at the workplace of my good buddy Blanc. The building is a charcoal color, uninviting and exclusive—a financial institution. I call Blanc and wait for my old roommate, Travis, to arrive. Once together, we make our way like giddy schoolboys to our hotel, check in, and go straight to the room. A knock on the door, and we open it to find our friend Williams standing there, party necessities in hand. "Let's go!" we yell, just happy to all be back together again.

We shower and get some food—pizza because I don't eat much else—before preparing to see everyone. Our suite consists of two rooms: one with a bed, and the other with a couch. We are young and naive and eager for adventure. We start the night off with drinks while we all get dressed into our usual going-out clothes: a button-down shirt, chinos, and lace-up shoes. Another knock on the door. Enter a couple more guys and a couple more girls. Now the pregame is starting. Finally, we're ready to leave.

We walk to a nightclub, laughing and ready to have fun. We step inside, and the stench of the spilled booze immediately hits us. Red lighting is supposed to make you feel warm and friendly, but really it just reminds me of infrared. The place is packed with people whom I hope never to see again. We do a couple of laps and then find our friend who bought a table, a pricey venture that the rest of us cannot afford. We say hi to all the usual suspects—some friends, most acquaintances. After a while, the night takes a turn. Williams is acting strange and then goes missing. Travis and Blanc are out doing their thing, but I am worried, enough to go looking for Williams. I find him outside peeing on the club wall (which makes him laugh hysterically), but he's way too drunk to be left alone. I grab him, and we take a cab back to the hotel room. Once we're back, Williams asks me, "Have you ever tried a hallucinogen?" I look at him, surprised. "Wanna try one now?" he prods.

I give it some thought and then say, "Yeah, might as well. I'll never get the chance again anyway." I had heard hallucinogens could alter people's perspective, so I hope it could help with my depression—that's how I justify taking it. So Williams and I begin our adventure. Whoa!

The hallucinogen hits after thirty minutes, and immediately we start looking at the art in the room. The shapes move and swirl; every color is vibrant. This is not what I expected. I am in complete control of my body, and my mind sees vivid pictures. Then everyone else gets back to the room. We laugh hysterically because we took a hallucinogen, and no one else knows. One of the guys is trying to get lucky with a girl, so the rest of us do what any guys who aren't getting laid on New Year's in New York do: we go to a strip club.

Now the hallucinogen is really kicking in. Once we get in, I don't really know what to do, so I just follow my friends and do what they do. I pull out twenty dollars from the ATM, intending to get a drink because I don't like private dances; they kind of freak me out. That could've bought me half a glass of water in this place. So I go back and pull out a hundred. I sit down and have visual distortions that are way too much for me to interact with people, so I just sit back and watch. I don't want any of these women touching me; I've never been a fan of strip clubs. I can't help but laugh at their costumes and ridiculous ploys to actually seem interested. The lights inside actually look quite cool. Neon lights. Nothing like the previous club's, though ... no infrared. I stay until everyone is content with whatever it is they got out of the place, and then we finally return to the hotel.

Once we get back, we find two more girls in our room who weren't there before. We stay up all night, talking about life, boys, girls, society, neuroscience, finance—the works. We stay up until seven in the morning, laughing about how good we all have it in the grand scheme of things. We "heart NY," is how we put it. We eventually fall asleep, but the hallucinogen is still impacting my mind. I can't sleep. I feel invincible. That is until the next day, when I experience the downside of taking a hallucinogen.

We stop to get lunch, some bagel shop, before returning to Connecticut, to Blanc's house. We laugh about our night and reminisce about how ridiculous we all are when we are together. While in the car, Williams says he has leftover hallucinogen. We are all horrible influences on each other, but yet we're very high functioning. He dares me to take some more, and since nothing awful happened the first time, I do. We get to Blanc's house. To our surprise, his entire extended family is there for a dinner. Williams and I are tripping and giggling at everything. Not good in front of a large Southern European family—I'm talking grandma and grandpa extended. His mom keeps plying us with food, and I'm beginning to sweat at this point. The seafood his mom makes is divine, though. Blanc, Travis, and I are sitting at the table, laughing hysterically, when all of a sudden I start to have a bad trip. I become paranoid and think his family has found out that I am high, so I start sweating profusely and tell Blanc we have to leave—they are keeping it together much better than I am. They even laugh at me because they aren't experiencing what I am experiencing. Blanc is confused but obliges. I later tell him his mom had to have known because of the comments she made. Blanc informs me that was all in my head and that his mother had scolded him for arguing with his brother, not for the fact that we are all tripping on something. We make it out alive, just barely.

We then head into the city and get another hotel room for the night. We all take my Adderall, a fine example of prescription drug abuse, but I can't keep up any longer. I tell the guys I can't go out, so I stay back in the room, and that's when true hell sets in. I'm left to be on my own as requested, but what I do not anticipate is the impact the mixture of drugs has on my sleepless mind. It begins to attack itself. I'm convinced that I'm going to die. I look myself in the mirror, crying at the person I have become. I never wanted to be a guy strung out in a hotel room by himself. My lowest point—that's what my brain is telling me. In reality, I'm okay; I'm just really tired. One of the guys wants to bring a girl back, so now I'm really screwed. Where do I go? What do I do?

I become "brave" and put in my ear buds, get my jacket, and leave. I just walk and walk. I do not say a word to anyone; I just walk. The cold, foggy, New York air fills my lungs, and I slowly exhale. *It'll be okay. Pull yourself together, Donald.* I log about thirty blocks in total. I do a lap around Times Square before making my way back to the hotel room. I take in all the lights, smells, and sounds the city has to offer. I see all of the Broadway play banners that blaze brightly in Times Square. I walk past countless people all too busy to see me or notice that I'm having a mental breakdown from a bad interaction of substances and sleep deprivation. New York is such a big city. I see all types of people, most of them smoking cigarettes and walking dogs, even after midnight. The city that never sleeps keeps me company while I cannot sleep. All the while, I can't help but wonder what am I so afraid of? What is so bad? Why had I cried and thought the worst was happening? Why did I sink so low? I have no answer. It is in that moment that I have an epiphany, or an emotional awakening. I think I have finally cured my depression and anxiety. I had been at my lowest point and found a way to keep going. It didn't have to be much; it just had to be one step at a time. Same goes for life. No problem is too big so long as you go one step at a time. I think I am cured. Turns out it was just the hypomania talking. The roller coaster has left the station and is beginning to pick up speed. I return home a different person.

Chapter 5
HYPOMANIA

I left the shelter of academic life and higher learning only to find myself lost in a world where extremes governed everything around me. New York had changed my state of mind, and I wanted to ingest everything, news in particular. We were clearly heading for disaster—economically, socially, spiritually—and no one seemed to care. Or so I thought. No one questioned the status quo.

My mind is going a million miles an hour. I have not experienced this mental clarity before. People around me don't seem to enjoy the opportunity we now have to acquire knowledge about things we *want* to know. *I want to know everything now. My friends and family don't fully understand the good they have in them. I think everyone has untapped goodness in them. They have dreams they don't believe they can pursue*—these thoughts race through my mind when I return from New York. The depth of my fear for humanity scares me. Hypomania does that to you.

I had maintained throughout college that my phone was broken and I could not make actual calls, I could only text. Which is a great excuse for not calling a girl—or my mother. However, this is important. I am frantic, so I call my mother in the middle of her workday. "The world is screwed up!" I tell her, nearly hysterical. "We have to do something!" I am practically in tears. What is going on with me? Why do I feel so overwhelmed? Probably because my brain is overactive. Ideas for making the world a better place, businesses of my own I'd like to start, books I wanted to read all come flying at me at once. So I begin to write. I start a blog on WordPress. I post my thoughts on Facebook. I send my writing, via e-mail, to everyone I knew. The problem is I am ranting—very unlike me. I push hard. I confront. I am brutally honest about myself and about others. I am sending clips of my hypomanic writing to old friends, to former bosses, to old professors. I want people to wake up, realize their potential, and give everything they have. *Right now.* I tell myself I finally have a voice. In reality, I'm making a fool of myself. Here I am, this normally reserved, quiet guy who suddenly starts ranting about society and life. What the hell do I know? I am only twenty-two at this point. I then collect articles of interest and share them on a channel I create on Slack, which is a group-sharing platform. I try to get everyone to respond, to think, to share their own articles and interests. I want everyone to exercise their brains the same way I am. I buy brain games for my roommates and me to play—chess, Connect Four, and Katamino. I buy books about all kinds of topics and make sure they are in our living room back in St. Paul where I live with three former high school buddies. None of them know why I suddenly have all of this energy and confrontational angst.

Instead of inspiring anything constructive, I end up offending everyone and digging a big hole—rather embarrassing as I look back. I try everything to get my friends to interact more with each other and rely less on the TV. Never mind that I love TV. Hypomania is like that. It bustles in and takes over your mind, your conversation, and your behavior. It's almost like an alter-ego. You feel untouchable, like everything is going right. It leads to an eccentric personality, and you become super-outgoing, hypersexual, and have enough energy to read, write, work out, and work endlessly. In fact, during this time, I used an app called Bumble to pick up women I normally would never have gone out of my way to contact. And this is very common behavior when you have untreated bipolar.

Chapter 6
COMING HOME

My parents insist that I see a psychiatrist. I definitely need one at this point. While they are relieved that my depression has lifted, they are concerned about my current condition, as they should be. I walk into the psychiatry office and immediately feel shame. *I'm not crazy*, I tell myself. *I can't be; this is just a misunderstanding. The psychiatrist will tell my parents that I'm still me, that I just have more energy.* I am finally out of my depressed shell. I fill out multiple papers pertaining to my mental health, and of course I answer spritely that I'm doing amazing. I don't even know why I need to be here. These forms are so ridiculous, as if a simple nine-question form can provide enough useful information to gauge a person's mental state. I grow angry at the redundancy of all of the registration paperwork. I finally hear, "Donald?" and follow the balding man with a stern face and large nose back to his office. I walk into the psychiatrist's office and see a plethora of degrees and a man with the stoicism of someone having his picture taken in the 1800s. He gives me the once over and doesn't say a word. He then asks a few questions and astutely reports that his preliminary diagnosis is bipolar of some sort. Probably something genetic. I come from a long line of geniuses with mental conditions of all types, so I suppose this makes sense.

Whatever the cause and whatever the condition, everyone around me is freaking out. Me? I'm the happiest and most productive I've ever been, oblivious to the chaos I'm leaving in my wake. I continue to write scathing blog posts calling out anyone involved in finance and those content with the status quo. I even try my hand at sexually explicit creative writing, sort of *Fifty Shades of Grey* for my generation. I send lengthy texts professing my love to a girl I'd had a crush on for years. None of what I'm saying makes sense. All the while, I keep asking everyone for feedback. I believe I'm writing a manifesto of sorts that will grow somehow in its profundity the more people interact with me about it. It doesn't occur to me that my mom finally relents and agrees to my begging for a dog (which I'd been doing for years) because she knows that I'm about to find myself very alone and will need a companion. Enter my first impulse purchase: a dog, Watson.

One of my idols is Sherlock Holmes, so naturally my faithful sidekick must be named Watson. I go online and find a notable candidate. He's a German Shepherd/Rottweiler mix about ten months old. He's gentle and wise beyond his young age. Watson, née Shea, comes from an overcrowded animal shelter from northwestern Minnesota, a leftover from his litter. I decide to rescue him.

I do a lap around the shelter before finding Watson. I hear the cries from all of these dogs in their cages, wishing I could adopt all of them. I see so many blends of breeds, all with pain in their eyes—kind of like the array of depressed people I know in my life. I want to save everyone. The worker there asks me if I want to see Watson in a closed room. I oblige and have my first up-close and personal meeting with my first ever dog of my own. I look into his eyes and see his relief at being chosen to go to his forever home. He probably sees an over-excited, fast-talking, twenty-two-year-old. I bring him home and introduce him to my roommates. They all love him. I am relieved and ready to have the responsibility of caring for my dog.

My Watson is a smart boy. Wiser than me by far. I try this new thing with him where I decide I don't want to domesticate him. I consider Watson as an equal. He is an extension of me. I do not control him. I only guide him in ways that I believe will benefit him. Watson came potty-trained. Doesn't bark. He never has bad intentions. Sometimes he does bad things, and instead of telling him to never do them again, I voice my discontent. But I make clear that I still love and respect him. I tell him it is okay to growl and get mad at me. So long as he remembers that I will overpower him at any point I deem necessary. But I would rather it not come to that. I give my dog the capacity to be himself. I have consciousness; therefore I am smarter than him by definition, but I only try to guide him to be free like me. In my hypomanic state, I think I am conducting some revolutionary state-of-the-art hybrid pet parenting.

Turns out my time with Watson would be short. He had picked up a deadly lung fungus in northwestern Minnesota prior to joining me—it's called blastomycosis. We took him to the vet. She gently informed us that he likely would not survive. We could try expensive medication, but the odds might not tilt in Watson's favor. Still we tried. Each day he grew weaker. Finally, his feet started to swell. I asked my mom to take him to the vet because I didn't have the courage to do so myself. I knew when she took him, he would not return. His blood wasn't circulating. It was for the best. But, I couldn't bear the loss. We only had a month together. My mind spiraled further out of control. And rather than face my emotions, I chose to get another dog. Enter Leonardo Wolfgang.

Chapter 7
OUTDOOR GAME WEEKEND

My friends from college see my rants on Facebook, get my e-mails, and grow worried for my mental health, so two of them decide to visit for my birthday in February. Blanc and Travis fly out from New York and immediately notice that something's wrong with me. I'm bouncing off the walls. I'm not sleeping. A lack of sleep just makes my condition worse, but I don't care. I have so much energy. I take them all over the place: to the Mall of America, to all the best bars and parties. We have a blast, just like the good old days, except I'm not the quiet kid I once was. I'm the life of the party. At least in my eyes I am.

The mania has slowly seeped in; I just haven't come to terms with it yet. Once someone is hypomanic, the next step is to become manic. If you have never dealt with this disease before, as I had not, you don't realize you're acting crazy until everyone around you can't stand you. No one fully understands how mania works; research is still in primitive stages. One fact is clear, however: not treating bipolar can be deadly. I must insert here that I didn't like the psychiatrist or his medication, so I had stopped both a couple of weeks before. His prognosis was off the mark—I was not on my way back down from hypomania. When I last saw him, I had just euthanized my dog and was suffering from the flu. Contrary to his observation, my particular roller coaster is still speeding upward at a rapid pace.

However, I don't have time to worry about my state of mind right now. Minnesota's first outdoor NHL game—Minnesota Wild vs. Chicago Blackhawks—is coming up, and I have bigger concerns than my mental health. That's what I tell myself. I get tickets for a bunch of my friends since it is my birthday gift and a once-in-a-lifetime experience. The weekend starts with the alumni game. We had tickets for this game between former Minnesota and Chicago players too.

I give my friends all of the jerseys I own so they can be dressed for the occasion, and then we make our way over to TCF Stadium on the University of Minnesota's campus. We soon realize our seats aren't together, so we head to the top-level halo seating and all pack in up there. We take pictures, bask in the sunset, and watch the North Stars/Wild[2] handily defeat the Chicago Blackhawks—I even get to see Mike Modano score a goal. Afterward, we go to a local bar and continue to celebrate the big win and taunt Blackhawks fans, all in good fun, until we inadvertently start a fight.[3] I'm late to the skirmish. I attempt to break it up and tell my friends to leave, and then apologize to the Blackhawks fans. I wrongfully get mad at my friends, and they get mad at me for not having their backs. In my manic state, love is a recurring theme, and I believe that my friends are above violence. Turns out they did not initiate the fight; they were defending themselves. At that point, I decide I don't have time to deal with this, so I call my mom and have her pick me up and bring me to my car.

While at the bar, I decided that I would make a documentary about the whole outdoor hockey weekend experience that would put Minnesota on the map. I just needed a GoPro for the next day so I could interview people on camera, asking them what they love about Minnesota and its status as the "State of Hockey." So I borrow one from a friend and return to my place, where I find my friends sitting on the couches waiting for me—almost like an intervention. I get into a shouting match with them over what happened and storm off to my room. Blanc then comes up and tells me I'm losing my friends and pushing them away. All the while I'm thinking I did the right thing by walking away. I cave in and apologize to my friends so that game day can run smoothly and so I can have them be in my video. The plan for my documentary was to record the day using the GoPro and then send the video to a friend in film school in LA. I'd then post it online, hoping the Minnesota Wild would see it and ask me to use the film with their promotion efforts. Another wild thought inspired by the mania. I am starting to have delusions.

---

[2] Minnesota's original NHL team was the Minnesota North Stars, so the alumni game featured players from both teams.
[3] Bipolar patients tend to have over-activity in the amygdala, a part of the brain associated with emotional reactions, originally thought to be associated solely with fear and anger, now associated with more components.

We wake up—well my friends wake up; I never actually went to sleep—and get ready for the day. I again let all of my friends borrow jerseys, and we have a few beers and head down to the game. We go to the local Buffalo Wild Wings where a friend working for an energy drink company helps us get into the VIP section—perfect. More stimulants and more free beer. We drink some more and take in the experience and the ambience while I get all of the moments on the GoPro. My friends get mad at me and tell me to enjoy the fun, but I can't. I think I have to make this documentary because when else can you get your team's first outdoor game on footage? I am losing it. We head over to the game.

We get in and find our seats. We watch the national anthem and US Air Force Thunderbird jets fly over in formation. Less than a few minutes into the game, Minnesota scores its first goal en route to a 6-1 rout and a very satisfying win. However, after the first goal, I inform the friend I'm sitting next to that I can't keep going—my heart is giving out from the lack of sleep. I have been taking norepinephrine reuptake inhibitors to give myself a synthetic adrenaline rush for six days in order to make the video and entertain my friends and guests. It's the drug truck drivers take to stay awake—or anyone else who has late-night shift work, to provide context. I take a cab ride home (cheaper than an ambulance) and collapse on my parents' couch. My dad, a doctor, and my mom—the compassionate one—tend to me and ask what they can do. My dad then gets me a beta-blocker to slow my heart down because I'm worried I won't wake up. I finally fall asleep and miss numerous phone calls from my friends.

The next day, I feel better and return to my place. However, things continue to escalate. My behavior oscillates between normal and violent. I believe I'm going to play for the Wild or at least be on the team's bench as I skate at a local rink. My delusions of grandeur are beginning to increase. I break my stick over the benches—because it has a curve I don't like. Whenever anyone challenges or questions what I say, I grow angry and start to shake. I believe I am becoming like God and that everything good around me I helped make happen. In my worldview, my parents draw closer as they work to help me. In my head, my friends bond together in their effort to handle me. Everywhere I look, I see people as happier—I think because of me. I think I can unite everyone in their efforts to save me, and by doing so, I think I am saving them. I think I am the next step in human evolution with the way my brain is firing.

Blanc returns home, but Travis stays behind so we can go watch his team, the New York Islanders, play my team, the Minnesota Wild; it's a regular arena game this time. Our seats are down near the glass, next to a friend of my parents. I talk to this friend, Doug, the entire game, and he is amazed at my brilliance—he hadn't seen me years. I believe he is going to pay my way to medical school because he has the money, and my parents do not. I also recognize one of the Wild's ice girls who had been one of my coaches at a youth hockey camp. Doug calls her over to introduce me, and now that I'm twenty-three, no longer a child, she gives me her phone number. I don't call her—I want to be mysterious and hard to get.

The next day is my actual birthday. I meet my mom at a local coffee shop and smugly tell her that this whole thing has been a research project that I had planned well over a year ago. I wanted to prove to people that they have good in them, and I tell her everyone proved me right, based on their efforts to help me. I admonish her not to tell anyone. And then I proceed to do so myself. My brother is beyond pissed—how could I put our family through such pain and strain?! He stops talking to me at that point. He had already blocked my text messaging because my constant rants were costing him his job. My parents are puzzled, not entirely convinced, but prefer deceit to actual illness. That charade lasts twenty-four hours.

Paranoia then joins grandiosity. I am sure someone on Facebook is threatening my life so I need to leave town. In truth, my mom told me to take down my posts, that I would compromise my future if I did not. So I pack my bags and head to Alaska because I have family up there. I want to make a fresh start. They have no idea what's in store. Neither do I. With that being said, let the film roll.

Chapter 8
MOUNT MAGNIFICENT

If the people around me had watched *The Big Short, Interstellar, The Martian,* and *Limitless* a few months ago, they might have seen where I was going. At first, the themes merely influence my interests and heighten my social-action passions, but then I begin to believe I am in these movies. That's when it gets scary.

Let's start with *The Big Short.* Wall Street greed and making money at the expense of others fuels my passion for helping the middle class to find an affordable way to invest. This leads to my startup idea to build an app that would allow us to round up each credit or debit card charge to the nearest dollar, sending the change to an investment pool shared by a group of friends. Sort of like a fantasy football pool, only we'd each earn dividends based on what we contributed. I plan to call it Change-Up. I also start day trading using an app called Robin Hood and do remarkably well, although that will fade because it's all about the long game. Now that I have decided to not immediately pursue medical school, I have the freedom to consider other options. And I discover I have a real knack for investing … but want to do so ethically.

Another theme I play with is starting a new society on Mars, inspired by *The Martian*. Not as crazy as you think—reputable science groups say it's possible. And I am convinced we're heading for annihilation on Earth thanks to those in charge of business and public policy to date. I truly think I am going to one day be a doctor in space. I even submit an application to Tesla to work there in order to get my foot in the door with its founder Elon Musk so that I could go to space. One of his many companies is involved with space travel. The craziness types out the whole application for me. (I later also test drive a Tesla car and almost buy a $100,000 Model D because I think Musk has tailored this vehicle especially for me.) I had read his autobiography, hence the origin of these thoughts. I also had a friend who works for Tesla read over my application—I haven't heard a word from him since.

Add to the mix my newfound ability to run my brain at full-speed and on all cylinders. Just like Bradley Cooper, the main character in the movie *Limitless*. NZT is a drug that lets the user function with a brain at full capacity, hence the name *Limitless*. Cooper starts off as a writer and then goes into investment banking (do you see the parallel here?). But what happens when you do too much too fast? Your brain wears out. The people literally work themselves to death. There is no balance. Why does Cooper survive and thrive in *Limitless*? Because he adapts. He finds a way to titrate and buffer his dosage so that he can gradually taper off. I'm not ready to do that yet, but I think I am functioning like someone in *Limitless*. If you look at the CT scans (computerized tomography) of a manic person, you will see various regions of the brain lit up, much more so than in the average person and starkly different from a depressed person.

I feel like my brain is finally operating at 100 percent. I see so much that others don't see. I try to share my visions, but the people around me only hear words, and they can't understand what I mean. I grow angry and anxious. I sound like a lunatic. Still, I don't want to find my own balance yet. At one point, I even tell my mom that I've created a pill that allows me to function just like Bradley Cooper. I think a combination of my norepinephrine reuptake inhibitor pills mixed with Oxycontin has made my brain fly at this capacity. I also find a cure for Alzheimer's too while I am delusional in my mania (again, an Oxycontin concoction). My grandmother had died from complications of dementia, and I missed her terribly, hence the thoughts. I see connections between things and events. I see how everything is related, almost like John Nash in *A Beautiful Mind*. I even write on the windows in my sun porch, using them like a white board, to connect all of my ideas. I start to leave what I call breadcrumbs for my friends and family, so they see too. Just like in *Interstellar*. I like movies, if you can't tell. In fact, I place particular books strategically where family members will notice them. I give them as gifts even though they aren't mine to give. I prod recipients to remember why these stories are significant. At one point, I believe that the dead communicate with the living through photographs. This plays with the idea that we don't understand our subconscious behavior, but the dead may influence it. I also postulate that dark matter, the matter we cannot view, is where dead souls go. (I had just read *Dark Matter and the Dinosaurs: The Astounding Interconnectedness of the Universe* by Lisa Randall.) Really weird stuff. They humor me, and we share some laughs, but they don't understand. Then, I buy a fitness watch that tells me everything. In *Interstellar*, two of the main characters use their watches to communicate with each other between dimensions. I believe someone is trying to talk to me through my watch. This watch experience nearly kills me.

Another symbol used in *Interstellar* that I take personally is when a book about Charles Lindbergh falls from the shelf. I've recently learned all about Lindbergh and his one-way trip out of Minnesota to escape the notoriety surrounding the kidnapping of his child. Lindbergh also happens to be the namesake of Terminal 1 of the Minneapolis/St. Paul airport. I decide that this Lindbergh connection cannot be a coincidence. It must be a sign. I get on the next flight up to Anchorage and arrive the same night. On the first leg, I tell the guy next to me that I'm writing a book soon to be available at his local bookstore. Then I give him my copy of *Dark Matter and Dinosaurs*. He's intrigued, but the guy next to him can tell I'm nuts. My story changes on the next leg of my trip. This time I tell the people next to me that I'm a medical student taking time off to produce a documentary and finish my book. One of them is a public speaking coach who invites me to speak to her class—she actually knows my aunt and uncle in Alaska. My cousin picks me up from the airport and is unable to tell I'm bat-shit manic at this point. He needed only to ask my flight companions.

I tell him about my epiphany on the airplane that love must be some sort of dimension since it defies space and time. I believe love is the way that people live forever, much like a hippy movement. He thinks it's such a cool take on life that he's blown away, not sure what to think. At least that's how I take it in my manic state.

I stay with my cousins who have three teenaged boys, all involved in hockey. I convince these kids that I am God. I keep asking everyone questions, behaving as though I have all of the answers. I am so jovial, people don't know what to think. The next day, I go to my aunt and uncle's coffee shop and sit down next to a young boy with autism. I play games with him; we read together and talk about his favorite parts of the story.

I actually think I'm healing him, going so far as to touch his head when I leave.

I go up to Alaska thinking that people will read my story, a collection of all my hypomanic and manic work, and want to talk to me. I'll be famous, and I don't want the attention, so it'll be cool to hide out in a little brewery as a famous person off the grid and tell my story. I maintain this facade long enough to get trained as a bartender, kind of, and get to work at my cousin's microbrewery. All the while, my mania is becoming worse. I can't sit still. I'm bouncing off the walls, and no one has really said anything to me yet. Then my first shift comes.

I have all this pent-up energy. I keep changing outfits, thinking that I am "parading the apparel" of the place, but really I just can't sit still. I switch between wearing jerseys (the brewery has a sports theme), to a mechanic shirt, to a hoodie, to a short sleeve, each one indicative of the job I am doing. Mechanic shirt goes on while I'm doing the dishes, the sweatshirt when I'm out and about, and the T-shirt when I'm serving the beer. All the while, no one says anything to me. I must have looked like a raging lunatic changing that much. I then see all of these ingredients in the beer and begin my mission to create the perfect beer. I believe I can use my premed knowledge and my newly acquired beer 101 knowledge to create the perfect beer. I begin to highlight ingredients and think about including molecules such as dopamine and serotonin in this drink, which is not possible, as far as I know. I think I can create the best beer ever, and it will be here in this brewery, where I, the famous novelist, will be hiding out from the publicity and everything will be perfect.

I make a symbol. I begin writing it on dry-erase boards all over the place. The symbol is simple: A delta on top of a bottomless triangle. The same symbol I used for my company/app idea, Change-Up. My cousin asks what it's about, and I explain it and still no questions are raised about my mental health. I'm manic, and people are eating it up. However, that is very short-lived.

At one point during my shift, I just leave without telling my cousin, which makes him mad. I walk straight toward a nearby military base with barbed wire and think that the government is spying on me.

When I return to continue my shift, the violent aspect of the mania sets in, and I yell at a customer. I maintain that he is spreading ignorance and that cannot be tolerated. My cousin pulls me aside and says, "If you ever pull that shit again, you're out of here."

I then get into a screaming match with him and tell him, "I quit." I storm out and begin to walk home. Furious, he sets off after me. I, in my manic state, refuse to accept that clearly I am wrong, given that it is his business, and I, the new guy, his family member, have behaved like a royal jackass. I continue walking, and he tries to pick me up, but I curse at him, drop my phone and wallet, and run away. I wander around Eagle River and begin to associate colors with my thoughts. Green signifies hope. I see it everywhere and decide I will go to the top of Harp Mountain to meditate and discover the secrets of life. But something drives me to veer toward my aunt and uncle's house. My uncle finally finds me.

"What's going on, Donald?" my uncle asks.

I look him dead in the eyes and claim, "I believe I'm God." He is confused and continues to probe and ask more questions, and I continue to maintain that I am God. He says I'm not acting like myself and that a police officer would like to talk to me. Enter a police officer. "How are you doing this evening?" "Just fine," I say. I explain what happened, and he asks if I'm willing to spend the night in a cell. "If I have violated any laws, then you are free to arrest me," I calmly reply, knowing full well that I haven't done anything illegal, just shameful. I am left alone and free to go home. Now I'm scaring everyone around me, and nobody knows what to do with me. So they call my mom.

My mom gets on the next flight to Anchorage and meets me at the Ted Stevens International Airport. I'm giddy and excited to see her. I still have nervous energy and want to go shopping. She has the money. I want to spend it. We go around town, and she takes me to several stores before catching on that she may potentially be enabling me. She knows I'm manic, but is unaware to what extent I have fully lost contact with reality. I think that all these stores are having special sales specifically for me. This bizarre thinking begins when our server at lunch has the same name as my ex-girlfriend's sister, leading me to conclude that my ex-girlfriend is a puppeteer of sorts, behind the scenes, creating these great gestures to win me back. I comply. I buy shoes, a camera, new clothes, and various other items because what do manic people do? Recklessly spend. All the while I'm thinking to myself that there is some diabolical plot happening and that there is some unknown person making this all possible because my life is just too perfect right now. Everything is happening just how it is supposed to, and I cannot be wrong. After the shopping spree, I stop again at my aunt and uncle's coffee shop to hang out with another cousin's child. He's playing computer games, and I begin to suspect that the government is trying to send me messages through the Internet. I also believe that since my start-up idea is taking off, that the government is keeping an eye on me to be sure that I'm doing everything ethically and legally. So, I look at every security camera and computer monitor to show that I'm behaving above board.

When we return to my aunt and uncle's home, I'm still a bundle of nervous energy, and that's when I decide to go on the scariest adventure of my life.

The weather is just right for a hike, so I think. The air is crisp, the snow has yet to settle and there is ice everywhere, but not too cold. I begin the trek up Mount Magnificent behind my aunt and uncle's house in Eagle River the same way I start most journeys that go badly: alone. My timing is awful. I leave the house at 8:30 p.m. It's dark out, except for strings of Christmas lights still shining their brilliant colors from trees and fences. The ascension is enough to scare some away—the mountain is thirty-two hundred feet up—but not me. I cannot follow the roads because they're too icy. It's winter, albeit a mild one for Alaska; temperatures are in the upper twenties. However, with the wind chill, it feels like below ten. So instead, I do what any insane person does and take the path less traveled, straight up through the woods. I claw my way up and grab onto branches and thorns in order to get higher and higher. I begin to heat up from the exercise. In fact, hypothermia is starting to set in. I take off my jacket so I'm now down to my sweatshirt, sweatpants, tennis shoes, and some wool socks. I keep hiking farther up. It doesn't occur to me that the hibernating season might be short this year thanks to early thaw. My mind begins playing tricks on me, and I believe my smart watch, an impulse buy I made earlier that day, is encouraging me to go farther—dangerous. I think there is something waiting for me at the top of the mountain, that people are waiting for me. Climbing this mountain is some feat for me to complete in order to prove my worth to get my ex-girlfriend back. Looking back, the origin of these thoughts came from my music playlist.

I keep climbing higher and higher and trudging through the snow and forest in front of me. All I can think about is the line from the Frost poem, "and miles to go before I sleep." I think I have to make it to the top by midnight, almost like Cinderella, so I literally do not stop once on the way up, making record time. I now think I'm acting in some movie, method acting because of my brother who's an aspiring actor. Again, I think my ex-girlfriend is the director behind the scenes because of her job with the movie industry. I expect to be airlifted from the top of the mountain once I arrive, and that all sorts of famous people and rich donors are watching my journey through a live feed, everyone placing bets on me as a means to raise money for my start-up idea. I have to prove to them that I am a worthy CEO. And my ex-girlfriend is behind it all, helping me make my dream come true.

Then I reach the top … and nothing. Not even any noise. My phone and watch have died from the cold. I chuck them both in dramatic fashion, thinking it will make for a perfect ending to the movie/live stream. Then my thoughts begin to race from one to the next. First, I consider descending down the backside of the mountain to go into hiding and then start a new life, basically faking my own death. So, I hide from every plane I see, thinking it is a search team out looking for me. Then I think cameras are set up around the mountain and that NASA is watching to test me for going into space, and that they manipulated conditions to make it as hard as possible for me. My thoughts don't make any sense—they just fly from one to the next. Then I think my family and my ex-girlfriend are waiting for me at the local hockey arena to celebrate my adventure. Whenever I feel like I can't take another step, I keep in mind my "reward" that awaits me.

Eventually, I come to the horrible realization that I climbed too high and I cannot go back down the way I came. I am screwed. I am alone. This is when I realize that I was oh so wrong. The mania had evolved into a psychosis. I'm left on a little plateau at the top of this mountain to think about what I'm experiencing. There are no lights, no sound, just cold wind and snow. I know I can't go back the way I came, so I decide to go down the backside of the mountain. I begin yelling for help and inadvertently start a mini avalanche. I am getting thrown by waves of snow and grab on to the nearest rock as I tumble down the backside of the mountain. No gloves. I pee on my hands to prevent frostbite. The snow passes. I begin to roll all the way down the backside of the mountain, hoping to get to the valley at the bottom to get water. I am freezing at this point. So I shake violently to keep my body temperature near 98.6 F. I realize I need to find oxygen soon because I am hyperventilating from the cold. I make my way to the nearest bushes. I curl up into a ball and begin expelling carbon dioxide. I realize it and need more oxygen, hence the trees. I also remember a lesson from one of my human physiology courses about how shivering helps warm you up when your body temperature drops. Hopefully the shivering will buy me some time. I make a faux cabana to protect myself from the wind. It's a pain at this point. I think this is all some test that I need to pass for NASA or for a movie plot. I probably deserve a B- right now for outdoor skills because I can't find the resources to build a fire. I roll all the way down until I hit the freezing glacier water underneath me, but I need water to survive. I had only had pizza that day. (What else is new?) I fall into the frigid water and immediately the freezing cold takes over. I now think to get up and find a shelter for protection, and I have the sad realization that I am going to die cold and alone. I begin to pass out. I float outside of myself, hovering above my body. The thought crosses my mind, *You've done this before.* Not sure what it means. That's when I see the light, so to speak. That is when my life flashes before my eyes, and for some reason I am spared. I don't know how or why, but for some reason I am still breathing. I begin to come back to life. Now the survival instincts kick in. Fight or flight. I have to fight like hell to live through this. Fight I do. I crawl all the way back up the mountain to get to a point where a helicopter can find me. Finally the light from the sun comes out. The next day is beginning, which means I will be found soon. All I have to do is hold out. I lay there passing in and out of consciousness until I hear it. The helicopter. I muster up the energy to whistle and wave my arms. They see me. They land off in the distance, and I walk toward them. I am finally saved. The scene was like Rose in *Titanic* whistling for help or Luke Skywalker in the *Empire Strikes Back*. So what's the first thing my heroes do? They take a selfie with me. I can't help but laugh, because I survived, and laughter is the only way to cope with the hell I just went through. I guess miracles actually do happen.

The State of Alaska wanted to retire the chopper because of budget cuts—apparently I am the first person they found alive in the past three years. I was able to use my college education of human physiology and medical anthropology to save my life. If God exists, he must be a goalie because that was a clutch save. I will never forget that experience and that brush with death. That was my turning point. There is nothing like an out-of-body experience, when you hover outside yourself and look down at the corpse left on earth. There is a short window when you can decide to leave it forever or you can frantically inch your way back. I wasn't ready. So I clawed my way back.

Part 3

THE EFFERENT SIGNAL—TREATMENT BEGINS

Chapter 8
CITY HOSPITAL AND RAMSEY

So I call the mania the fire, much like renowned author and psychology clinician Kay Redfield Jamison does. What happened after they found me, frozen from the knees down, was nothing short of a miracle. The Search and Rescue Team took me home to my aunt and uncle's. I slowly and painfully peeled off my ice-laden clothing. I took a hot shower and changed into clean, dry clothes. I still hadn't admitted to myself that I truly had bipolar. I thought I was getting rescued and was going to the hospital to recover from frostbite and any other injuries I had suffered from acting in the so-called movie—not because I was mentally ill.

Then the police put handcuffs on me, put me in the back of their squad car, and took me straight to the local ER psych ward, which I refer to as the penalty box. It was protocol. Rightfully so. I almost unintentionally died. I fit two of the three criteria necessary for law enforcement to commit someone for evaluation and subsequent treatment: I was a danger to myself, and I was mentally unstable. They brought me to City Hospital's twenty-four-hour lockdown unit in Anchorage for evaluation and, most important, to restore my meds. At that point, I started to get concerned. Once inside, I began to see more connections. There was Watson's desk, with a delta as the symbol. The mania raged on.

I am kept in a small room with only magazines to entertain myself. I cannot contact the outside world. The wallpaper is beige, like every other hospital room, and dark; but mostly, it's lonely. The medical staff leaves me to think about my actions, as if thinking is the issue here. Thinking is what I need to *stop* doing. If I describe the mania as a fire, I will call what happens after the mania the ice, and I am freezing. I realize that I am no longer thinking like myself and something or someone else has taken over. I cooperate at the hospital. I take all the meds they give me, just hoping that I will be allowed to go home. I'm not. I sit there answering questions about what I was doing. Was I aware of my actions? No. My purpose was not yet fulfilled, and my life was spared, so that is how I answer. I tell them no, I did none of this intentionally. I tell them I believe I have become manic and need help. An aside here: while I'm in lockdown, I see a guy dressed as Goku from Dragon Ball Z. Sorry, I try very actively to repress these memories. I just thought it was ironic since Goku was my childhood hero. Conclusive diagnosis: bipolar 1 with severe mania.

I return to Minnesota on a low dose of Abilify, but the mania continues. I think I have solved the Bitcoin (virtual currency) equation, when really it is more mania. Here we go. I "discover" that Bitcoin could work by having one Bitcoin per person in the world in case capitalism fails. So the price of Bitcoin at the time of my discovery was $420. Multiply that by 21 million, the maximum amount of Bitcoins in circulation, and you have … the population of the world. Except my math is wrong, and I'm off, substantially. My brain is going a million miles a second, so I do not stop to check my numbers. That's when I think I have figured out the money equation. A kid I had been working with on my app idea has a lot of Bitcoin, so I tell him my discovery and think we are rich. Well, really *he* is rich, but I want to sell him my app idea, so I think I will be rich too, which ends up annoying most of my friends, and I even lose a few.

My friends are happy I'm alive, but I'm clearly not right, and they are afraid of me. I return to my parents' house to live, but when I visit my roommates, they call my mom to come get me. No one wants to associate with crazy. So after this, my behavior starts to turn toward attempts at reckless spending. Nothing too unreasonable, just a house in a new development and the Tesla I mentioned earlier … Jesus. Good thing my mother is there to stop me or I would be in a lot of trouble. So after that, I decide to go back to a hospital for help.

I voluntarily check myself into St. Paul Ramsey's ER and psych ward, or what I call the penalty box, thanks to the lead of a friend who had been there before me—a short, buff, tattooed guy who had experienced much of the same thing. One conversation with me and he offered to drive me to the ER himself. He wouldn't take no for an answer, so I called my mom to take me in. I didn't realize I'd have to wait to get what I needed, like waiting-in-line-at-the-DMV long. Overflow forces me to hang out for almost twelve hours in the ER before going to the limbo second floor, where I join convicts, schizophrenics, and other mentally impaired people. The rooms are on the perimeter of this unit, with a large common room in the middle, much like a prison. There are games and coloring books dispersed throughout the common room. There are about seven other people in the penalty box who look much more intimidating than me. It's here that I meet Derivative.

Derivative is my boy. He is my Morgan Freeman as we plan our escape like in *Shawshank Redemption*. Derivative is a man who keeps talking about uniting the 'hood. I agree. He keeps blaming those East Side boyz. I'm just south of the West Side myself, so I can't help but agree. You have to have a sense of humor to tolerate these places, so I am a thug for a day.

I spend the first night in this holding pen and feel the mania taking over again. I am so bored; I need something to do. Derivative and I devise an elaborate plan to escape and get the 'hood back together. Eventually others grow interested. So I play games with all the other "crazy" people who are stuck in limbo with me. We draw and color. I school them in chess and Connect 4. I am clearly cognitively superior to 99 percent of this population, I think. I continue to see connections with games, coloring books, shows, people, and the like. I basically become the epicenter of this psych ward and talk to everyone, convincing them that they are not crazy at all. I was probably one of the sickest ones there at that point. However, everyone's eating it up. I make everyone question their own reality, and they begin to see me as sort of an authority figure. I even leave my telephone number so that all who pass through will be able to get in contact with *the* Donald Rodriguez, celebrated author. I even sneak my way onto a computer to check on my writing on WordPress.

There is one who challenges me, one whose intelligence rivals my own. Spencer. Spencer is good at chess. He has manic depression, just like me. If I am Sherlock then he must be my Moriarty. We start with chess. Too simple. We have to go outside the box … a board game called *Apples to Apples*. Now this is not a child's game. We're playing to win.

I eventually get moved up to the seventh floor, the real psych ward, when a bed finally opens up there. Little do the people working here know, I am only checking myself in so that I can see a psychiatrist, get the prescription for the meds I need, then be on my way … so I think. The seventh floor is much more pleasant, but still confining for a bipolar patient with PTSD (from the mountain). I know my brain has been screwed three ways to Sunday, but I'll survive because I have to. I essentially mess around with the staff and ask lots of questions because that's what a manic person does. They question everything regardless of how annoying it is. Spencer too makes it up to the seventh floor, and that's when we have our Seventh Heaven conversation.

Spencer and I discuss how we both had, in our manic states, considered the possibility that we were God or had communicated with God at least. I tell Spencer about how I believe that we are each our own God, that God is in each of us. I don't have a religion. Not even agnostic. He agrees that we are all God, creators of our own universes and realities, and that there are infinite universes for all of our infinite choices. Time is linear, we think, so we can only experience one universe. Spencer and I conclude that we must both be creators of our own universe and our own realities, that there are multiple other universes similar to the movie *Mr. Nobody*. (This is about the last remaining mortal man on earth who has to go back through his life to examine each decision he's made and how each choice leads to different outcomes as he tries to remember who he is. Hence our obsession with multiple universes and realities.) However, whatever we choose must be correct because we chose it. This is enough to intrigue our listeners. We get labeled with God complexes, and rightfully so. Then we have to take our meds. Humph. But before we swallow, we first contemplate an idea from *Paradise Lost*. Is the mind in itself a heaven or a hell? It depends on how you look at it. Perspective. We ultimately argue that heaven and hell are both here on earth since they are just ideas made up by people. We conclude that we both must be right and that, simultaneously, everyone else must also be right. There is no such thing as right or wrong; there is only choice and perspective. We present our argument to the in-house psychologist and kind of blow his mind with our abstract thinking. We realize we aren't getting the therapeutic conversation we want here, so we decide it's time to check out once we have the right meds prescribed. However, we aren't allowed to do so. Our doctors claim we need seventy-two hours at least. Ha. I will not be told that after I volunteered, so I find a way out (in retrospect, that was dumb of me). I find out what meds they would prescribe for me and then use that information so I can get better from home. My PTSD makes me feel trapped, which cements the decision.

I walk laps around the unit practically non-stop. I just can't sit still. Plus, I think that I'm smarter than the psychiatrist since I have unlocked the secrets to the universe and created a brain drug. My brain has evolved, and these people are here to dumb me down to their level. These are my humble thoughts.

I can't help but remember the mug from which I sipped my last coffee. It states, "Home is where your mom is." Quite true, mug, quite true. So my mom reluctantly agrees to take me home even though it was AMA—against medical advice. I don't give her any choice.

Chapter 9
HOME AND MY SLOW DESCENT INTO HELL

I choose to go home to get better because my father is a physician and my mother is a saint. Together they provide me with enough love to overcome all obstacles, so far. However, the depression of someone with bipolar is quite a new beast to me. Nothing like organic chemistry. Well ... kind of like organic chemistry. My mind has been firing at an unprecedented rate, so now it must recover and get lots of sleep. I am in a daze and unable to think, let alone write. The meds also make me this way because I haven't gotten them quite right yet. The words flow, but there is no continuity, no appeal ... just word vomit. It's not as much fun to write now that I have lost the fire. Therefore, I must be experiencing the ice—the deep, cold depression. What do molecules do when they're cold? They come together and form something solid, like a close family. *I'm coming down for the sake of my family,* is my rationale. I leave the hospital against medical advice because I believe I am a special circumstance. What I mean by that is the rest of the seventy-two hours I would have spent in Seventh Heaven would have been dedicated to learning coping skills. I know how to cope—so I think. The hospital psychiatrist tells me as much. I just need a gym, some open air, some books, and to be able to wear shoes with laces. I cannot anticipate that the depression will go on for twice as long as the mania.

As with all wounds, time is a necessity. Time is not something I like. So in order to heal, I am encouraged to sleep a lot and not think. I cannot stand this. It is a limitation to the mind. I miss my mind. I cannot tell whether or not my mind is drugged or if it is depressed. Probably both. I don't really know the difference between the two. I know that medication is supposed to help me, but I can't help but feel let down. I know the mania was wrong, but I prefer it to the depression. What a weird trade-off. Either I must be miserable (depression) or I make everyone around me miserable (mania). How do I win? Apparently lithium. At first that makes sense to me. I think of the brain as a battery. What do batteries run on? Lithium. I think of the body as the car (must be electric, not internal combustion, for this analogy, and besides, I want an electric car), so then who drives? Consciousness? I think the soul. Mind, body, and soul. So my body is healed. My soul is meh. What's left? My mind. My favorite thing about me is sick and plagued. What a curse. I will never be the same. I fear my brain will never work the same. All that effort I had put into building the facade that was me will forever be lost because the truth finally reveals itself: I am mentally ill. How do you heal a neurological condition? You can never heal it; it's a part of you for the rest of your life. You can only manage it. You can keep it at bay while the whole world goes about the same exact way. My condition allows me to see the world differently, though. It's something that society values, to some extent, if you can manage it. So does time heal a sick mind? Does medication? Can you ever actually heal a sick mind or is a mind sick because it does not fit in with the other minds? So how do I manage? I write. I'm writing this book to show the cycle of a manic-depressive mind. The fire and the ice. The ups and the downs. The mania and the depression. To encourage others to get help if they see themselves in anything I've said. Something my psychiatric nurse practitioner (psych NP) said really surprised me: "You're lucky you got help so early on. Most people suffer with bipolar symptoms for years before they do anything about it." Don't wait.

Depression slowly seeps in. It's like being a dog in a cage. You can see and hear the outside world but ultimately you cannot interact with it. All you can do is sleep. You try to be heard, but no one can hear you. Eventually you get let out of the cage, and you get a few hours to play if you're lucky, but ultimately you know you're going right back into that cage. Except unlike with a dog, depression is a cage for the mind. It's a prison you *choose* to occupy. Your brain makes the choice for you. Your one friend, your instrument of experiencing the world, locks you up and seemingly throws away the key.

I don't have much hope right now. I am scared of this loneliness and inability to function like a normal person. I am left with memories and a fear of the future and contempt for the present. My thoughts don't seem to be my own. They sound like a bad Oscar Wilde novel. How do I get out? How do I escape? I honestly don't know.

There reaches a point where I cannot get out of bed. I cannot face reality. I sleep sixteen hours a day. I find solace in sleeping because it allows me to escape reality. I can see and be with people who I presume do not ever want to talk to me again. I can live out scenarios I think are lost to me now. When I do wake up, I watch TV and I do not talk to anyone. I am suicidal every second of every day. I plan multiple ways to kill myself. Once the reality of everything I have done sets in, the humiliation, guilt, and stigmatization consume me. I think my life is over. I imagine hanging myself with a rope in the basement, but figure I can't do so because I don't know how to tie the correct knot and the rope I have is too short. I think about sitting in my idling car in the closed garage, but conclude that it might take too long, and if I get caught, I'd be sent back to that dreadful hospital. I contemplate overdosing on my pills, but soon realize they'll just make me sick, not kill me. I even research ways to kill myself without it looking like I have done so. I do my homework, but fortunately cannot settle on my method for departure.

Part 4

IT GETS BETTER

Chapter 10
THE POWER OF HEALING

I turn to biomedical treatment and traditional Chinese medicine (TCM) out of desperation and hope. I want anything for a quick fix.

Headaches dominate my life. They stem from medication side effects, recovery from severe manic activity, and sleep deprivation, along with withdrawal from all of my previous medication. I seek relief through acupuncture. I had learned about acupuncture while pursuing a minor in medical anthropology at my alma mater. A family friend recommended a specific doctor, Dr. Lu, to me. So I make my first appointment. If nothing else, acupuncture is relaxing and can help with whatever you are feeling, at least while you are there. I was skeptical about all the needles going in my body, but it never hurt. Basically if Po from *Kung Fu Panda* could do it, then so could I. I have never tried acupuncture before, but from what I'm told, it basically reroutes energy through channels in your body called meridians, which are out of sync. TCM is much different from biomedicine, mainly in the ambience and the tranquility of the patient rooms, but is similar in the number of Asians who practice the art form. While both have their pros and cons, I decide that I can just do both and hope for the best.

Every treatment with Dr. Lu has its totems. I walk in, he says hello, I say hello in return, and we go straight back to the procedure room. Along the way, there are many herbs and remedies, all with Chinese labels that I cannot read. I am even given pills that look like tiny cannon balls; I have no idea what they're made of. Whatever, I'll take them anyway; add them to the list. Dr. Lu leaves me to undress down to my underwear, and then I put on a polka-dotted gown. It's about as uncomfortable as a changing room at your local department store. Once I'm ready, he comes in and asks how I'm feeling. I tell him what troubles me and what I would like treated. He takes in the information and plots an appropriate plan. He then says, like clockwork, "Let us begin treatment," and proceeds to stick needles all over my body. He is quite calm for someone inserting needles in another human being. He normally starts with my head since most of my problems are neurologic, and then works his way down to my abdomen (for energy), and then down to my feet—each needle serving a different purpose. The needles do not hurt; they feel like an annoying mosquito bite or listening to someone from *Jersey Shore* attempt to speak English: just a tiny wince. The needles evoke specific responses, though. For instance, when he sticks needles in my frontal cortex, my thoughts begin to become a little bit different—more positive. He then turns on an infrared lamp and shuts the lights off and lets me rest for about forty-five minutes. I am left to my thoughts and to focus on my breath and other physiological things happening to my body. I am more or less motionless due to all the needles, so it is quite tranquil. After the forty-five relaxing minutes are up, he comes back in, turns on the lights, and removes the needles. There is seldom any blood, and if there is, it is negligible. I still don't get how that works. Then I get dressed and am off for my day. At the end of each visit, Dr. Lu reminds me to exercise.

My brain is not quite back to normal, yet I need something to do. I decide to work part-time at a local hockey rink, instructing high school goalies because I want to be around other insane individuals. I should point out that getting back to work is usually a long and cumbersome process. I started my new job while still partially manic and then progressively became more depressed. I basically slept all day up until I had to go to the rink. I would dread going because it was too much to see or talk to anyone, let alone coach. I was quiet and stern during this period, but now I've opened up and connected with the kids and staff in a much healthier manner. I am fortunate because my boss used to be one of my goalie coaches. I told him right away what was going on, and he's supported me throughout my time working with him. I doubt I could have held down any other job. Working has allowed me to focus on healthy eating and physical activity, which go a long way toward recovery. I neglected both for quite a while, and it was then that I experienced leaden paralysis, as I mentioned earlier. I literally could not get out of bed. It was as if I was in a comatose or vegetative state; I was that depressed.

My place of work does not offer your typical workouts, though. These workouts are endurance training, high-intensity interval workouts. They're not for the faint of heart. Basically, how it works is that your body is fighting itself and against gravity. Barely any weights are used; it's all about isometric holds. Isometric means the joint angle and muscle length do not change during contraction. Furthermore, there is one other workout method that some do that involves electrically contracting specific muscle groups, which also serves as neurological stimulation and modulation.

The coach does not believe in running or sport-specific exercise; instead he promotes propelling force in the correct athletic position. One should be able to absorb and propel force (like getting hit and hitting) in correct athletic position. One should know how to contract and simultaneously relax agonist and antagonist muscles. This type of workout requires mental and physical fortitude, so I push my limits as much as I can. This workout is extreme, and any type of exercise that makes you feel better will help. Whatever gets you moving is what you should do.

I found just taking that first step and turning it into a routine was essential. When I stopped my physical activity, my mood tumbled downward. But then I would push myself again, forcing myself to do what I really didn't want to do, and that has helped my healing process tremendously.

I start every workout by nervously gulping as the coach, Sar, comes in ready to give commands. He looks like Dolph Lundgren, the Russian guy from *Rocky IV*. The man is intense. The workout room smells of sweat, and there are never more than ten people in there. Pictures of all the former athletes who have gone on to play college and professional hockey line the walls to serve as motivation. I work out with all age groups. I prefer the younger tiers because I actually look strong next to them. When I first started, I could barely do the workouts. That's how it is when you're depressed, though—no energy. I was kind of like a sloth. Over time, I've gained both physical and mental strength.

If you have nothing else, you at least have the workout to give your all to or at least a fraction of your all. You can drown out the depressing stuff and just zone in on reaching your exercise goals. However exercise is not enough to fix one's mental game.

Another means of helping the depression is behavioral therapy. My therapist surprised me at first; he was not like my psychiatrist at all. There was no plethora of degrees, no hostility, and no stoicism. He even sat cross-legged on his chair and wore sandals. The first time I walked into his office, I noticed his sculptures, paintings, and photos, all of Eastern origin I presumed. I encountered tranquility here similar to that with Dr. Lu. We introduced ourselves to each other and made small talk just to get the conversation going. I suck at conversation when I'm depressed and can't shut up when I'm manic—he's dealt with both. I met him when I was experiencing hypomania. That evolved to mania, followed by depression, so he has seen the full spectrum of my disorder. In my depressed state, we do a lot of Eastern practices, such as breathing techniques and yoga—stuff that I used to hate doing, but I'm pulling out all the stops at this point.

I notice that whenever I speak, my therapist is very cognizant of my body language. He also talks about channeling of energy and is pleased that I see an acupuncturist. I am able to talk freely with my therapist about whatever is ailing me during that particular time, and that too helps. I don't feel like being there half of the days because I'm stubborn and hate opening up, but I force myself to go (and there is a stiff cancellation fee). It's useful because when your mind is plagued by depression, you only see the dark, whereas a therapist can see the light and remind you of it. He or she helps you see beyond the void. Furthermore, that person can help you see more of yourself than just the depressing side when you can't. Eventually I appreciate my therapist's efforts to help me make lifestyle changes that ultimately lead to my stability. He teaches me how to correct my negative thought patterns into self-loving ones and create mindful awareness. I had years of practice ruminating over self-loathing thoughts, especially during this past year. He offers my mind refuge in our work together.

My therapist reminds me of my future, whatever that entails, and all the promise it holds. He tells me that I can do anything I put my mind to once it is healed and once I can find the right combination of medications, along with routinely applying proper mental hygiene and using the coping mechanisms he has taught me. He also recommends I take a multivitamin, vitamin B complex, Vitamin D, and DHA (a fish oil supplement). So now I'm taking the works, and they do help. All of these practices in conjunction serve a purpose: to make one feel better. I cannot say how each fares on its own, but I know that together they all help me get closer and closer to that ever-elusive target range that is homeostasis.

Chapter 11
HOMEOSTASIS: GETTING BACK TO BASELINE

I still struggle with putting the pieces of my life back together. I have setbacks. I start to gain confidence and energy to reconnect with my friends and to explore career options, and then I regress. I fear my friends liked the old me and won't be too keen on who I am now. I find obstacles to pursuing some sort of medical career every place I look. It's just the fear. I don't know when I'm going to go off the deep end. I feel like I'm living with a secret or hiding something and that it's just going to come out. It's definitely perpetuated by the bipolar. I am in this constant state of uncertainty and fear because I don't know my limits. I don't know when the mania or the depression is going to come back. Every time I've had a goal that I've worked for in life, it has been taken from me, and I'm afraid to start again. Injury crushed my hockey dreams. Now, bipolar likely will prevent me from becoming a doctor. I'm afraid that if I don't have a perfectly routine and outlined life, then I will turn crazy and hurt people. I grow frustrated with how foggy my mind is, and I can't decide if it's lingering depression or the medications themselves, so I stop taking them for a while to see how I feel.

Turns out, I feel worse. There are days when I cannot stand the thought of seeing another person. I stop working out. I eat too much. This heightens my anxiety, and I become a recluse. I have enough sense to tell my mom that I am not taking my meds as often as prescribed. Her nose tells her I haven't showered or washed my clothes recently. My silence on the way to and from my psychiatrist appointment unnerves her. I don't have the energy to shower. I sleep all day, watch TV, and reminisce about how good my life used to be. I cannot get outside of my own head, and I figure I will either hit rock bottom and bounce back, or I will hit rock bottom and die from the fall. Either way, I am forced into action.

When my mom wants to meet with me, I put her off. Then I skip a therapy appointment. This prompts a surprise visit from my mom to my apartment. I refuse to let her in. I send her a text instead. "Why are you here?" She is nothing if not blunt as she texts back, "Because you smelled like a homeless person who hasn't had a chance to bathe the last time I saw you. You keep putting me off and you skipped your therapy appointment. You do realize there's a stiff fee for that, right?" I ask her to give me two more days. She agrees and sets up another therapy appointment, during which she will join me. She offers to pick me up to be sure I attend. I had resumed taking the Lamictal after that meeting with my psychiatrist the week before, and now I feel so much better. Another lesson learned: Always be completely honest with your psychiatrist and therapist. They cannot help you otherwise.

I have finally reached a point where I can accept that I have a disease that will require lifelong maintenance, but it will not deter me from my goals. I have decided I do still want to work in the medical profession and possibly go to medical school. I'm learning more about what I must do to pursue this career, and I know it won't be easy. I have come to accept that I will likely have to keep quiet about being a person with bipolar 1 when applying to school. My story of survival will not win me points with any admissions committee. However, I'm learning that I must not let fear of failure ruin my life. I have a dream, and I need to see where it goes. So, I prepare for the GRE first to see how I cope with testing before I attempt the MCAT. Maybe a master's degree in science makes sense before I attempt medical school. I'm finally employing structure and routine in my life without question or resentment, to stave off further bipolar episodes and to help me get to where I want to go. I realize I'm better off moving back home while I continue to work part-time and prepare for school. Less isolation. I'm getting the hang of the lifestyle changes that will help me be healthy: sobriety, yoga, a nutritious diet, medication, meditation, regular sleep … and patience. And having a spritely little dog to keep me company helps too.

I am lucky to have friends and family that will help along the way. I just had to be honest with them and say, "Hey, this is what I have." Those who care about me still respect me and do not stigmatize me. Not everyone stuck around, but those who have truly understand. So long to the days when I would care so intently what everyone thought about me. "Be who you are and say what you feel because those who mind don't matter, and those who matter, don't mind." A wise man, that Bernard M. Baruch, adviser to Franklin D. Roosevelt.

It will never be easy, but it's necessary in order to get off the bench and back on the ice to play another shift. It always helps to tell your own story so that others can find their own form of homeostasis. Who knows, you might even get a fan or two.

Part 5

A WORD WITH MOM

Donald did not arrive in this world with an owner's manual, and I sure didn't have one when he began to display signs of bipolar. Looking back, he started to behave differently months before he reached his peak in Alaska. Normally an introvert, Donald was outgoing and confident, really quite the conversationalist interested in a broad range of topics at Thanksgiving and Christmas. *He's finally come into his own,* I thought. *We're getting to see who Donald really is.* Then the trip to New York, a Christmas gift from us. He returned a different person. Very open and honest ... to a fault. He told me about his experience with a hallucinogen—I was appalled, of course. It's that hypocrisy whereby we revere the artists and inventors who, while under the influence, create amazing work for us to use and enjoy. John Lennon's "Imagine" immediately comes to mind. As do Apple products. Yet we freak out when we find out that our kids experiment. At the same time, if he truly was no longer depressed, I could get behind that.

But then came Donald's frantic phone call to me. I understood his concern about society's future, but not his intensity. He called his older brother, in tears. "What's wrong with me?" he sobbed. Donald's older sister had speculated that he was on the high end of a bipolar episode when she read his texts to us while on his way home from New York, gushing about how happy he was and how much he loved us. I thought she had been unnecessarily cynical at the time. Now, I began to believe her.

My entry into Minnesota's mental health system felt like I had plunged into the icy waters of Lake Superior without a life jacket: cold and unforgiving, with few options or opportunities to survive. I soon discovered anything I learned would be on my own. First, there was the matter of age: Donald was twenty-two, soon-to-be twenty-three. I couldn't force him to get help. In fact, several places I tried wouldn't even let me make an appointment for him. Second, if I *was* lucky enough to find a clinic that would allow me to act on Donald's behalf, the psychiatrists' practices were closed to new patients or they had no openings for months. Donald's father is an endocrinologist, and he persuaded a psychiatrist to whom he referred many patients to evaluate Donald, even though this psychiatrist's practice also was closed. I managed to line up a therapist at the same clinic, so we thought we were on our way to making things right. Donald agreed to go to appease us. But he had to stop taking all medications, prescribed and otherwise. We all knew lab tests would reveal traces of marijuana, something that could heighten manic symptoms, but not cause them. Donald told us he used it occasionally to calm down. We needed to know if anything else was interfering with his health as well. Was his mania caused by chemicals or by bipolar disorder?

I learned quickly about manic behavior firsthand. I understood Donald's desire to make the world a better place—after all, we are an activist family. I did *not* understand the irritability, aggression, and complete disinterest in anyone else's point of view. I grew concerned at his public social media stream-of-consciousness writing. And there was no substance to his flight of ideas. No "how we're going to get this done" aspect to his proposals. At the same time, I enjoyed his intellectual growth and his eagerness to get family and friends to read, think, and act.

The first meeting with the psychiatrist did not go well. This was not going to be a good fit. Patients who are hypomanic like their state of mind, they're so relieved to leave depression behind them. This psychiatrist practiced from a place of tradition and authority. I expected someone with his level of experience to be able to cut through the manic behavior and guide Donald in the direction he needed to go. That did not happen. The psychiatrist prescribed a very low dose of an antipsychotic drug called Abilify "to be sure Donald didn't become more manic." *More manic?* This can get *worse*?! My concern—and everyone else's—was the crash back into a deep depression. It never occurred to us that he could get more manic first. We left with absolutely no information about the medication prescribed, why the psychiatrist chose it, or anything else about a possible diagnosis for Donald. Hypomania seemed about right, but the laboratory tests would tell. I had no idea what questions to ask. I didn't know what I didn't know. Donald was to call the psychiatrist in two weeks to report on the effectiveness of the medication. And then the psychiatrist was going out of town, so the next appointment wasn't for another month. Too much time between contact and follow-up. Lesson learned: find someone who has the time to manage care closely while sorting out diagnosis and medication regimen.

Donald took the Abilify for a while, even tried taking it at night since it made him foggy during the day. And then he stopped taking everything. His friends grew more concerned for his wellbeing. Friends and family kept insisting that we get Donald help, hospitalize him if possible. No one could understand that we could do *nothing*. He was an adult. We would have to wait until he was a danger to himself, to others, or disabled. Meanwhile, I read everything about bipolar that I could find from reputable medical websites. Friends whose lives bipolar touched began to share their stories with me. I'd had no idea up to this point that bipolar was part of their family fabric. I learned how not to antagonize Donald. This skill eventually put me in the position of sole caregiver. His friends weren't aware enough to understand what the bipolar disease entailed. They complained of his lying, his grandiosity, his aggression. I tried to explain the difference between lying and telling the truth as opposed to delusion and reality. Donald really believed everything he was saying. Don't challenge him and he won't become aggressive. I cared for my mother who had dementia during her final years. I learned from my experience with her how to handle someone who wasn't operating in reality. Because of her, I understood why Donald tried to self-medicate in so many ways—something that's very common among people who suffer from bipolar. In my mother's lucid moments, she would beg me, "Please fix my head!"

I was literally biding my time until I could get Donald the help he needed. His dad and I thought that moment arrived when Donald showed up on our doorstep midway through the NHL's Wild/Hawks outdoor hockey game. He was finally truly scared, heart racing; he couldn't sleep. We should have brought him to the emergency room then, but figured we could get him help more quickly on our own rather than wait hours in an ER. Wrong decision.

The only good thing at this point was Donald truly connected with his therapist. And I had the phone numbers of all his key friends so I could hear their concerns and urge them to do what needed to be done to keep Donald safe. Basically, I conducted damage control behind the scenes. Still, Donald's symptoms continued to worsen. His roommates couldn't tolerate him anymore, and I had nowhere to put him. He wouldn't come home, that I knew. He insisted on going to Alaska to stay with my niece and nephew. I figured my Alaska family had better psychiatric connections than I did, and Donald deeply respected my nephew, so maybe he could persuade Donald to get help. With that reasoning, I cleared Donald's stay with them and then brought him to the airport.

Not more than twenty-four hours after he landed in Anchorage, we got several calls from my brother-in-law. Donald picked a fight at my nephew's brewery, ran off with my nephew's truck, and now was missing. We urged my sister's family to call the police. Maybe *now* we could get him to a psych ward for the help he needed. Not to be. They did call the police after finding Donald walking back to their home, but Donald appeared to be "just fine" according to the officers, so charging him with anything would have landed him in jail, not the ER. That meant I had to make an impromptu trip to Alaska to retrieve my son and figure out what to do.

Donald was all smiles and agreeability upon my arrival. Yes, he'd come back to Minnesota to live at home. Yes, he'd take his meds. Yes, he'd see a psychiatrist if we could find one that was holistic. The next day, all bets were off. That's the challenge of living with someone who suffers from bipolar—they change their tune every day. There's no malicious intent; it's just that's where they are at any given time—at least when they're manic, and sometimes when they're depressed too.

Then came the trek into the dark night. My sister and I gratefully agreed to let Donald go out for a walk. He was really getting on our nerves, and he needed to expend his volatile energy. He'd been obnoxious and aggressive most of the day. He'd spent a fair amount of money using his credit card that fortunately we shared, and the limit was low. We knew there were many lights on around her home, which is perched on the side of a mountain. We figured he'd wander about and then come back in. And then he didn't.

I will say that I'm glad that the crisis we all were waiting for happened in Alaska, where there was one law enforcement jurisdiction and the officers have extensive mental health training. Had it happened in the Minneapolis/St. Paul area of Minnesota, the outcome would have been dire. My sister called the police after two hours with no sign or communication with Donald. They arrived quickly and took action immediately. They deal with a lot of mental illness in Alaska, so they knew what to do. I know many people around me gave Donald up for dead. I tend to not believe the worst until it stares me in the face, so I remained steadfastly hopeful.

I didn't feel anything, just confident he would come back alive until I heard otherwise. Long story short, the law enforcement and rescue team of professionals and volunteers (and dogs) found Donald fourteen hours after we reported him missing. He shouldn't have been alive, but he was.

The officers in charge told me more about how to deal with someone suffering from bipolar than any other professional had up to this point. They encouraged me to take our time before we had them take Donald to the ER. I just wanted him checked in before anybody could say otherwise. I didn't realize that we would not be able to see him, that he literally would be locked up, but in a psych ward, not a jail cell. For him, there didn't seem to be a difference. He also didn't understand about the need to use an area code when calling me in Alaska—and no one in the hospital explained it to him. So, he ultimately felt abandoned by us, although that was not our intention.

Anchorage hospitals have a twenty-four-hour hold rather than the seventy-two-hour hold we have in Minnesota, but it was long enough to get him settled to go home. And they discharged him with a definitive diagnosis: bipolar 1 with severe mania. However, here's where I nearly lost it as a parent. I called Donald's primary care physician to get a required referral to a psychiatric adult day treatment program within her clinic's system. She provided the referral reluctantly, explaining that normally a Minnesota physician would have to see him display his manic symptoms in the ER. That because his crisis happened out-of-state, she doubted the hospital program affiliated with her clinic would accept her referral. And she hadn't seen him in a couple of weeks either. In short, the health care system protocol interfered with her being able to do what was best for Donald. I wanted to scream, "Are you fucking *kidding* me! My child nearly died during a severe manic episode, and he is supposed to follow up with care at home, and we can't make this happen?!" She did try to submit the referral, but, as she predicted, the healthcare system denied it. Turns out the outpatient program I wanted didn't deal with bipolar, just anxiety and depression. Seriously?! His PCP did tell me that a mental health urgent care center of sorts did exist, and if things got bad, I could take him there. I could not believe it. Let's wait for yet another crisis and then get help. The Anchorage hospital wouldn't prescribe anything either; we had to use the few tablets of Abilify that Donald had left to tide us over until we could find someone who would see him. And we still had a six-hour flight between Anchorage and Minneapolis/St. Paul to navigate. Fortunately, we had a tailwind, and arrived home in just a little over four hours. Still, Donald had to get up and walk around a few times to calm down. And I started to watch all those movies that had motivated his behavior.

Upon our return to Minnesota, I found a psychiatric nurse practitioner (psych NP) that would have time for Donald. I actually only had three options in the entire seven-county Twin Cities area—one psychiatrist and two psychiatric nurse practitioners within our particular clinic system had open practices. The psychiatrist and other NP were a good forty-five minutes to our south. I had the sense to suggest using the existing referral that had been denied to secure this appointment with the psych NP. Still, even there, no one provided us with any information about how to provide the best care as a family member to someone with bipolar. In fact, Donald had to sign a waiver to even allow me to attend his appointments with him. We *did* get some practical references from the short stint Donald had at Ramsey Hospital when he checked himself into their psych ward. He didn't qualify for any of their outpatient programs either. The psychiatrist there thought he just needed a medication adjustment. I didn't like the idea of Donald leaving Ramsey against medical advice, but I understood his inability to tolerate lock-up for an undefined amount of time. Again, I couldn't prevent him from leaving. I agreed to pick him up because I wanted him to be at home, not somewhere on the street. Fortunately, his appointment with the psych NP was the next day. And she referred him to a psychiatrist colleague when his depression showed signs of suicidal tendencies. That psychiatrist ultimately took over his care. We would have had to wait six weeks for an appointment with a psychiatrist upon leaving Ramsey. So, we're on a long journey to sort out what meds make the most sense for Donald. We think we've found the right cocktail for now, after much tweaking. But even that may have to change as needed. It's a lot like people with diabetes who must keep a log of their blood sugar levels to determine how much insulin to use.

No one has mentioned support groups; just a passing reference to the National Association of Mental Illness, a useful resource on many levels. Our clinic system offers nothing specifically for bipolar patients. Depression and anxiety are the focus. It's pretty hard to have a meaningful conversation with someone when they're manic. I met with Donald's therapist to learn about how we as a family could best help Donald. Even here, I had to get Donald's permission. I am struck by how many hurdles family members must clear trying to learn how to provide support to someone with bipolar—the one thing that person needs most from us. The therapist gave me information that would help me teach Donald's siblings and other family members how to connect with him. I had to help them get past their anger at his manic behavior and understand what it means to have bipolar 1.

Depression hit Donald hard. He kept asking for information that would provide him hope. I came across a useful quarterly series called *BP Hope*, an online and print publication of stories and information for people with bipolar and their loved ones. I also ordered a book called *Break the Bipolar Cycle: A Day-by-Day Guide to Living with Bipolar Disorder* by Elizabeth Brondolo, PhD and Xavier Amador, PhD.[4] These tools help Donald and me figure out what questions to ask both the therapist and psychiatrist. They help us track his symptoms and give us both ideas for how to maximize whatever energy and capabilities we have at any given moment. Donald's complaint of memory loss motivated us both to do *more* research, and that's how I learned that achieving a return to "normal" was not just about concocting the most effective medication cocktail to address the extreme highs and lows. The moods and the medication both can cause cognitive compromises. Typically, tweaking the medication dosing helps, but it's hard to know if the mood or the med is behind the symptoms. Then there's the working through the grieving process. This was by no means a straight line. Some days Donald was clear and positive about his future. Other times, he fell back into lethargy and feeling nothing at all. This is why therapy has been so important—cognitive behavior therapy in particular.

I stay close to Donald, gauge how he's feeling, and nudge him in the appropriate direction when the time is right. I listen, ask questions, and learn as much as I can so I can help him rebuild his life. Even this attentiveness isn't always enough. I had no idea of the true depth of his despair—not until he told me. Ultimately it comes down to time. That's

---

[4] A list of all of the books we read to help us cope is listed at the back of the book.

what everyone told me, and now I know it's true. Today Donald is stable, working toward a life in hockey management or medicine.

What do parents do who don't have the resources or connections or perseverance? Our mental health care system is broken. One piece of good news: the Minnesota Governor's Task Force on Mental Health recently submitted its recommendations for an overhaul of our state's mental health system. Increasing early intervention efforts, improving crisis response and broadening access to care are among the many action items. Until these recommendations become reality, we advocate and wait for better medications and greater access to care.

And we tell each other our stories. We help each other write a happy ending.

Afterword
EXCERPT FROM MY LETTER TO FAMILY

Dear All,

I am happy to say I am alive. For those of you who don't know or have been confused about my behavior for the past eight months, please let me provide an explanation. In January, I was diagnosed with bipolar disorder. At the time, I did not know what the diagnosis meant or what the condition entailed. I experienced a profound change in mood: almost incomprehensible happiness. I felt like I was on top of the world, and I began to take on projects, read ferociously, and finally came out my shell a little bit. Then I learned the hard way what happens next. You see, I was experiencing what is called hypomania, which given the prefix "hypo," is a prime description of what happens next: mania.

I began to become delusional. I lost contact with reality. I could not control my emotions or my thought patterns. I was revved up. I wanted to take on the world, and in my state, I thought I was God's gift to earth. I could not have been more wrong. My behavior was a burden to all who crossed my path, and I am just beginning to forgive myself for all the damage I caused as I hope you will all forgive me. For those who experienced me in this state, I give my sincerest apologies. However, out of all this, there is silver lining.

If anything, this experience has taught me the value of love, family, and life. To be honest, before all of this, I never really appreciated the idea of family or life. I knew the importance of it and the social utility, but I never really got down to the roots of it—unconditional love. What I mean by this is that despite all of my actions and words and hurt and confusion during my manic state, you were all there for me. It brings tears to my eyes just typing this because of how much it has meant to me—your compassion, your love, your willingness to be there for me, and most of all, your unyielding support. The aforementioned list is what has kept me alive in light of what happens after the mania: the most unbearable depression.

As you all know, in my delusional state, I climbed Mount Magnificent and was trapped up there overnight before I was helicoptered out the next morning. Badass, right? No, it was just the first level of hell. Not even Dante could prepare me for what followed: the deepest, darkest hell that the human mind can conjure up. After I was helicoptered out of there, I was sent to a local hospital, where I began taking medicine for my illness. Imagine a rollercoaster if you will. I had sped up to the top, peaked, and was now crashing downward, hence the hospitalization. I was shortly released and headed back to Minnesota to continue treatment and live at home in order to deal with the oncoming depression.

Bipolar depression is not like your average depression; it consumes you to the point where life becomes unbearable. I am lucky to be alive today and proud to say that I am doing better. I could not have done it without your help. You all reminded me of who I really was and constantly reminded me of how loved I am. I cannot thank you enough—it saved my life.

The tricky part about manic depression (bipolar) is that I will most likely have to endure these cycles again. My condition is not curable; it's something that will be a part of me the rest of my life. However, I choose to not let it define me. I choose to see it as a blessing. This disease has taught me so much about life, love, and the resilience of the human spirit. I choose to use all of the pain as something to learn from and vow to do everything in my power to never sink that low again. Whenever I am down, I am now comforted by the fact that *it does get better*. We all have our trials and tribulations, but what allows us to endure is the fact that it is not permanent. "This too shall pass," or whatever. I cannot begin to tell you how important that realization has been to me. Everything happens for a reason. Instead of saying, "How could this happen to me?" I simply say, "This happened. Why did it happen? What can I learn from this? How can I find the light when it is pitch black around me? How can I become a better person from this?" and then I move on because at the end of the day, life continues to go on with or without you.

Instead of living in fear, I chose to see fear for what it truly is: a natural physiological response in the face of perceived or actual future danger. It's your brain's built-in, annoying, protection agency. I am now able to harness that fear because I am blessed with one thing that can conquer it: love. I would just like to reiterate how grateful I am to each of you for blessing me with this gift.

Appendix
MUSINGS FROM A MANIC MIND

Getting to the Next Plane

What is the one thing that humanity has in common? Consciousness, and by extension, choice. You all have a choice. You can choose to be good or as bad as you please. Here is how my experiences during my time on earth all come together. So let us assume that life is like a game. The way to win the game is by being a good, honest, moral person. While this is subjective for each of us, so too is our choice to accept it as such. So humor me. Pretend we all had a morally good and intellectual friend, the architect, and then we had an annoying parasite friend who is like a vestigial organ: it exists but evolutionarily serves no purpose. God and the devil to some. I'm arguing they are one in the same. An idea. A choice. I choose to believe that having moral fiber and being a genuinely good person allows you to gather more currency for the next level of experience, the mind without the body. Transcendence. Enlightenment. The next plane. Those all focus on people being good. The architect and the parasite are trying to speak to us, to our subconscious, but too many of us are numb and cannot hear (try turning down the TV). There are so many who do good and enhance others' experience on earth, which, simultaneously, enhances their own. There is no currency higher than morality, unless it is introduced to an imbalanced system. I believe we are out of balance. Now here is how I think this game works. Once you realize your own idea, and that you have always been pointed toward both random chaos and balanced order, once you realize that for all that to happen, life cannot be a mistake. And then you can realize how precious life is. I think the more good you do, the more moral currency you rack up, and you proceed to the next level, next dimension, next place—you fill in your description of the divine here. Now some of you will say, "Well then why not just blow your brains out now!" to which I will respond, "You miss the point." That wouldn't make sense. Once you realize that life is a game, a dream, and you wake up, yes it is lonely. But it is beautiful. Can I still connect to my fellow man? Yes, because I view all of us as part of Team Human, all moving each other forward, because we are the good guys. For perspective, when good ideas are put to bad intentions, people die. Think of the Cobains and the Ledgers. They died because they understood themselves and their fellow human so fundamentally well that they grew scared that man would ultimately just kill itself anyway because of how messed up the current system is—cut-throat competition; no balance. When given the choice between life and death, they came to the conclusion that mankind is so far gone that they could not tolerate being a part of it anymore. Did they level up? Were they good people? I'm not sure; I'm fairly confident they were. Their deaths may have been coincidental or they may have been intentional. But when you do not have a choice, and life is taken from you, it is either because you have gathered enough moral currency to level up and move to a different dimension or you made a choice to be bad and will be reincarnated as a cockroach. I kid. But either way, it is not over. We cannot fathom death because it does not exist. If our minds cannot fathom it, then it must not be reality. But yet some of us feel like we can speak to or hear dead people. I believe that is love. Love is how we communicate with these other dimensions. I believe that love is the idea that transcends all bounds. We cannot fathom it either. We can only experience it. So with this in mind, I have a game to play. And for those who ask about money... Yes, when hard-earned and used honestly and with mutual respect, then yes, the ideology of money is good. However, when used for greed, it can destroy the world. We have choice. We have consciousness. It's up to you to exercise it, and Lord knows America needs some exercise. So ultimately what I am saying is, being good and moral is worth more than money, if you cannot find an honest way to balance the two. Life is all about balance. Life is all about you and, transitively, everyone else. Life is what you choose it to be because it is a finite experience that you have. The experience on earth comes to an end. It's all about what you choose to do with it that leads to what happens next.

Fear of the Uninformed

Hollywood has created so many stories that depict our lives, if only we could see the themes for what they are. For instance, here's one that I have come to conclude about our generation. It is afraid because it is uninformed. People fear what they don't know. We are ignorant because our news is diluted with ads and porn and evil and robots pretending to be human and people who aren't so much human as they are television characters. The news reminds me of a bad TV show nowadays. A really sad one. But there is still a silver lining. There is always optimism. Fear of the unknown is a choice. We are all scared of what we don't know, and we are lashing out as a survival mechanism. Humanity is at a crossroads. We will kill ourselves and everything else on this planet, and be the biggest failure in human history. *Or* we could finally be the generation to fix it—to realize that we are part of something bigger than ourselves. Will it be easy? Nope. Will it be fun? Not at first. But let's be the generation to make our mark on history, the generation that saved mankind. Let's not close the book; let's continue writing. Educate yourself, read, be yourself, be different, but choose to do all of these things because it is what you genuinely want. Find balance and peace of mind by doing what you want and doing what you don't for the sake of your better man. Be selfishly selfless. If anything, all my writing is intended for is to remind people that they have it inside themselves to be the change they want to see in the world (yes, like Gandhi). If you respect icons like Gandhi, then respect and embody their ideas, which were intended to enhance the human experience. Strengthen your own experience by understanding and forgiving yourself, and then allow yourselves to do the same for others, if you haven't already. There is so much good out there fighting alone in the shadows. Why not unite them? Try. Choose. Let yourself fail in order to find out how to succeed. Let's win this one, team.

So here I am hypomanic (not yet manic) and getting a little frantic. I feel grandiose and am writing with a hint of paranoia. I know, usually, that the situation is not as dire as I make it, but I want everyone to drop what they're doing and start caring as much as I do because ... well I'm hypomanic. It sounds like a plea, and in a sense, it is. However, people seldom respond to pleas without context, and no one knows my context at this point. I am like a child finding out Santa isn't real for the first time. I am crashing headfirst into the harsh reality of the real world after a four-year college career.

My love of the brain and the intense emotion, including love, caused me to write the following piece while still hypomanic.

Love is Like a Synapse

Love is like a synapse—I discovered this tonight. The way I thought about love was the same way I was taught to think about the brain. The brain is made up of specific connections that serve specific functions that only work when stimulated by a stimulus powerful enough to evoke an action potential. What if love is like a synapse? What if you don't stimulate it with a little thought? Does the synapse disappear entirely? No, how could it? Once it is formed, it cannot break, I think. We just don't focus on it or acknowledge it. It's just there—a part of us. It quite literally becomes a memory. It gets encoded into our minds and manifests and influences who we are, but if we do not provide it with adequate stimulation, then that connection fades. Now, over time, Tau proteins may aggregate, and those connections may be harder and harder to form. Then you get Alzheimer's, and you don't even remember who you are anymore. Crazy, right? Literally. But what if you could never stop that neuron from firing, no matter if you wanted to. (My grandmother, who I helped care for while she slowly faded from dementia, was able to remind me that she loved me, even when she couldn't pronounce her own name. That's something I will never forget or have ever admitted because it was such a personal and beautiful thing— such as how I viewed her existence in my life.) What if the synapse has so much plasticity that it is engrained into who you are? What if love is plasticity? That would make love subjective, right? That would make it like life—an experience. A privilege. An acknowledgement of the beautifully paradoxical symmetrical chaos that balances out as love. However, if love is like a synapse, then, like a neuron, its activity must oscillate. The frequency and amplitudes may be more frequent and larger than you always want, but it all balances out as homeostasis, as love. However, surely you cannot only have one synapse—you would die (how ironic). Yet, the more compassion and attention and respect and focus you show that synapse, the more likely you are able to fire that action potential that is love. Because that is what it feels like, right? A sensation that courses through your body that cannot be confined to the world as we understand it. Love transcends it. Evolutionarily, it doesn't make sense to love, yet we do. Well, an argument can be made for child-rearing, but I digress. Love would be considered a vestigial organ if not for the fact that it is more powerful than the confines of a single organ (the brain is an organ). Love is something to be cherished because it too is a finite experience, as is our existence during our time on earth. We choose to spend it with the one we love. The law of attraction. The particle you blew up next to during the Big Bang somehow became integral to another tangible, conscious being, such as yourself, regardless of race, gender, sex, anything. Love transcends it all, and the original attraction from the beginning of time finds a new context, a new subject. Because we are all just matter. And matter cannot be created or destroyed, right? I won't get into dark matter here. But love is beautiful when you discover it. Whatever shape it takes or whatever way you experience it, it will forever be a part of you because it is hardwired into your brain regardless of your choice. It is a memory, a stimulus, or something repressed. Nonetheless, love transcends choice, the one thing we all have. You don't choose the person with whom you fall in love. But you can decide whom you choose to experience love with. I know who has my attention and who has formed the most powerful synaptic connection I've ever experienced—love. If only I knew where to begin with her … I suppose I'll start by texting her to remind her that she's my other particle, and through the chaos that is love, she will always be a part of me. Or I could simply say "Sup babe?" I guess she'll see when I'm ready to get down on one knee and tell her, but only God knows when that'll be. I guess she'll have to back me into a corner—checkmate.

Checkmate

I never knew I liked chess. My dad always told me I would. I could not fathom how he could anticipate an entire game of moves based off of just one isolated piece placement. He told me to get Chessimo to learn. I did, and it helps me think about the world differently. Why is the game of chess important? Well, from my understanding, the game of chess was fairly popular until IBM's computer Deep Blue defeated some of the best players in the world, including Gary Kasperov in a six-game match. Why? Deep Blue "learned" a valuable lesson about life that his foes could not compete with—to play the odds, every time. Constant risk assessment. I think, to some degree, our subconscious has the storing and computing capacity of any computer; we just don't know how to use it because we don't know the language well enough. What is the programming language for humans? Probably math. While we have been busy taxonomizing, computers have been busy simplifying. As a result, Deep Blue quite literally learned from its mistakes, and played the odds, and adjusted constantly. Now the game of chess is less popular. Why? Because Deep Blue beat some of the best human players. A machine won the thinking game, for now. Why do some have contempt for Deep Blue instead of trying to understand why it won? Some of us do ask ourselves these questions. So now I know why the movie about Bobby Fischer is called *Pawn Sacrifice*. Because it is a bold strategy that people had not seen before. You quite literally sacrifice a pawn, right away, which somehow gives you an advantage. Now what is cool about chess is you can play the man, but there are limitations to the game that force you to play the game. However, with chess, there is always a move to be considered until, well ... there isn't one. Today I played a game that I both won and lost. I had played the first half hour and beat my adversary ... so I thought. We took a picture (because if you don't take a picture it didn't happen, so says my dad). In the picture, I noticed that I had actually not won. There was still a move that would allow my adversary to win. I pointed out that the game was not over, and he was eager to continue. I could see this as charitable and naive, but instead I chose to see it as real competition. Honest competition. Let's see who can actually outthink and outsmart the other man and win the best type of game, the mind game. I lost the second half of the game. It took in total about an hour and a half of pure planning, and to no avail (partially). I lost after all that planning. How? I had a strategy, and I let it get away from me. I got distracted. He bested me because he wanted it more than I did. I was content with the original pseudo win, and he wanted the revenge win. He got it. I can only encourage such acts of competition, and I can only encourage more to play chess. It's great mental exercise. I lost twice today, and I had previously only lost to one other person (who beat me while we were supposed to be paying attention to a physics lecture that we both already knew because we read ahead). But I lost twice today, once to the original party, and once to a fresh foe. Ultimately, both were good games, but my mind was exhausted. I loved it. The endorphins your body release from a brain workout are just as addicting as they are for Olympic athletes working out (and the rest of us squares). I learned a valuable lesson today, though. The long game is more important (stock market analogy here somewhere). The person who first beat me today was someone I was afraid could beat me; I was just waiting for when. I think that was his mentality too and that's why he beat me. So now what? Well, if I learned anything from Deep Blue, it's that for every mistake, there is a lesson to be learned. Constantly update yourself and your strategy and your tactics, and learn the game and the rules to win. Beat everyone in the most honest way possible: by out-thinking them. Not with manipulation, but anticipation. You can't change the rules of the game; you can only change how you play it. Such is life, right? So I have a prediction. I think a human who fundamentally understands his opponent (the learning computer) can ultimately provide a much better game. So what is my first opponent doing now after this mentally taxing day? He's playing the computer in chess.

My Own Starry Night

I live to play hockey. It helps calm me down when I get antsy. I just discovered an outdoor skating complex/park two blocks away from me. I just so happen to skate when all the kids are at school and all the old people are at work. Perfect. I wake up and get my body moving. The cold air fills and wakes up my lungs. My eyes water (damn those lacrimal glands) from the wind ... or is it joy? I don't know. I have fresh ice because they Zamboni at nine the night before. So I have a freshly frozen rink all to myself, in my backyard. My dream. But this all feels like a dream lately. It all seems too good to be true, but I've seen the light, and I can't unsee it; that's what I tell myself. I see the world differently now, forever. A mosaic, chaotically structured. I also now believe that people's subconscious communicate with one another—body language, intuition, survival instincts, etc. Why do teams win and not individuals? Teamwork, not individual work. What if you could rely on your fellow man to be educated and could see him as having a type of knowledge you either do or do not want to know? What if you could trust your fellow man to be your teacher and not hesitate to listen to him or her? I'm honestly asking. What if that could be true? How would we do it, people? I am better at hockey now than I ever have been in my life, and it's because I'm finally working smart and not necessarily hard. I anticipate the plays. I bait, I outwait, I outthink my opponent. I use my teammates as extensions of myself and communicate in the most effective way I can. Give them a target to pass to. Send the puck to where you think your teammate will be and guide him there. Do not yell or force him to do things he has no business doing. There is nothing immoral about being beaten. It is stigmatized under the pretense that we all have to outcompete each other to survive. Teams lose so that they know what it's like. You cannot learn how to win unless you learn how to lose. You cannot appreciate winning if you have not lost. No team is consistently perfect. It is not possible. It's honorable to try but irrational to obsess over an ever-fleeting ideal. I lost twice today in 2-2 hockey. It was the best hockey I personally have ever played. I did not want to win; I wanted my team to win. I made plays that were too advanced for my novice teammates and could not devise a winning formula. I relied too much on educating and leading by example and not on winning. We did not lose because we were bested. We lost because we chose to. We chose not to make certain plays or did not communicate effectively. We did not have the winning mentality, literally. If we had watched *Friday Night Lights* before instead of after then we might have had more luck. You know, "Clear eyes, full hearts, can't lose." I can tell you a lot about the body, but a psychiatrist is better for the mind.

Resources We Use

Brondolo, Elizabeth & Amador, Xavier. *Breaking the Bipolar Cycle: A Day by Day Guide to Living with Bipolar Disorder.* New York. McGraw Hill. 2008.

Emmons, Henry, MD and Kranz, Rachel. *The Chemistry of Calm: A Powerful, Drug-Free Plan to Quiet Your Fears & Overcome Your Anxiety.* New York. Simon & Schuster. 2010

Emmons, Henry, MD. *The Chemistry of Joy: A Three-Step Program for Overcoming Depression Through Western Science & Eastern Wisdom.* New York. Simon & Schuster. 2006.

Emmons, Henry, MD et al. *The Chemistry of Joy Workbook: Overcoming Depression Using the Best of Brain Science, Nutrition & Psychology of Mindfulness.* Oakland, CA. New Harbinger Publications, Inc. 2012.

Federman, Russ, PhD and Thomson, Jr., J. Anderson, MD. *Facing Bipolar: The Young Adult's Guide to Dealing With Bipolar Disorder.* Oakland, CA. New Harbinger Publications. 2010.

Ghaemi, Nassir. *A First Rate Madness: Uncovering the Link Between Leadership & Mental Illness.* New York. Penguin Press. 2011.

Hanson, Rick, PhD and Mendius, Richard, MD. *Buddha's Brain: The Practical Neuroscience of Happiness, Love & Wisdom.* Oakland, CA. New Harbinger Publications. 2009.

Hornbacher, Marya. *Madness: A Bipolar Life.* New York. Houghton Mifflin Company. 2008.

Miklowitz, Donald J. PhD. *The Bipolar Disorder Survival Guide, Second Edition: What You & Your Family Need to Know.* New York. The Guilford Press. 2011.

Ramirez Basco, Monica, PhD. *The Bipolar Workbook, Second Edition: Tools for Controlling Your Mood Swings.* New York. The Guilford Press. 2015

Redfield Jamison, Kay, Psych. D. *An Unquiet Mind: A Memoir of Moods and Madness.* New York. Random House. 1995

Made in the USA
Monee, IL
29 October 2020